# Dear Future Exam Success Story

First of all, **THANK YOU** for purchasing Mometrix study materials!

Second, congratulations! You are one of the few determined test-takers who are committed to doing whatever it takes to excel on your exam. **You have come to the right place.** We developed these study materials with one goal in mind: to deliver you the information you need in a format that's concise and easy to use.

In addition to optimizing your guide for the content of the test, we've outlined our recommended steps for breaking down the preparation process into small, attainable goals so you can make sure you stay on track.

We've also analyzed the entire test-taking process, identifying the most common pitfalls and showing how you can overcome them and be ready for any curveball the test throws you.

Standardized testing is one of the biggest obstacles on your road to success, which only increases the importance of doing well in the high-pressure, high-stakes environment of test day. Your results on this test could have a significant impact on your future, and this guide provides the information and practical advice to help you achieve your full potential on test day.

**Your success is our success**

**We would love to hear from you!** If you would like to share the story of your exam success or if you have any questions or comments in regard to our products, please contact us at **800-673-8175** or **support@mometrix.com**.

Thanks again for your business and we wish you continued success!

Sincerely,
The Mometrix Test Preparation Team

**Need more help? Check out our flashcards at:**
**http://MometrixFlashcards.com/SOL**

Copyright © 2026 by Mometrix Media LLC. All rights reserved.
Written and edited by the Mometrix Exam Secrets Test Prep Team
Printed in the United States of America



I0892292

Mometrix
TEST PREPARATION

# Virginia SOL Grade 5 Reading Secrets Study Guide

# Table of Contents

# Introduction

**Thank you for purchasing this resource**! You have made the choice to prepare yourself for a test that could have a huge impact on your future, and this guide is designed to help you be fully ready for test day. Obviously, it's important to have a solid understanding of the test material, but you also need to be prepared for the unique environment and stressors of the test, so that you can perform to the best of your abilities.

For this purpose, the first section that appears in this guide is the **Secret Keys**. We've devoted countless hours to meticulously researching what works and what doesn't, and we've boiled down our findings to the five most impactful steps you can take to improve your performance on the test. We start at the beginning with study planning and move through the preparation process, all the way to the testing strategies that will help you get the most out of what you know when you're finally sitting in front of the test.

We recommend that you start preparing for your test as far in advance as possible. However, if you've bought this guide as a last-minute study resource and only have a few days before your test, we recommend that you skip over the first two Secret Keys since they address a long-term study plan.

If you struggle with **test anxiety**, we strongly encourage you to check out our recommendations for how you can overcome it. Test anxiety is a formidable foe, but it can be beaten, and we want to make sure you have the tools you need to defeat it.



Copyright © Mometrix Media. You have been licensed one copy of this document for personal use only. Any other reproduction or redistribution is strictly prohibited. All rights reserved.
This content is provided for test preparation purposes only and does not imply an endorsement by Mometrix of any particular political, scientific, or religious point of view.

# Secret Key #1 – Plan Big, Study Small

There's a lot riding on your performance. If you want to ace this test, you're going to need to keep your skills sharp and the material fresh in your mind. You need a plan that lets you review everything you need to know while still fitting in your schedule. We'll break this strategy down into three categories.

## Information Organization

Start with the information you already have: the official test outline. From this, you can make a complete list of all the concepts you need to cover before the test. Organize these concepts into groups that can be studied together, and create a list of any related vocabulary you need to learn so you can brush up on any difficult terms. You'll want to keep this vocabulary list handy once you actually start studying since you may need to add to it along the way.

## Time Management

Once you have your set of study concepts, decide how to spread them out over the time you have left before the test. Break your study plan into small, clear goals so you have a manageable task for each day and know exactly what you're doing. Then just focus on one small step at a time. When you manage your time this way, you don't need to spend hours at a time studying. Studying a small block of content for a short period each day helps you retain information better and avoid stressing over how much you have left to do. You can relax knowing that you have a plan to cover everything in time. In order for this strategy to be effective though, you have to start studying early and stick to your schedule. Avoid the exhaustion and futility that comes from last-minute cramming!

## Study Environment

The environment you study in has a big impact on your learning. Studying in a coffee shop, while probably more enjoyable, is not likely to be as fruitful as studying in a quiet room. It's important to keep distractions to a minimum. You're only planning to study for a short block of time, so make the most of it. Don't pause to check your phone or get up to find a snack. It's also important to **avoid multitasking**. Research has consistently shown that multitasking will make your studying dramatically less effective. Your study area should also be comfortable and well-lit so you don't have the distraction of straining your eyes or sitting on an uncomfortable chair.

The time of day you study is also important. You want to be rested and alert. Don't wait until just before bedtime. Study when you'll be most likely to comprehend and remember. Even better, if you know what time of day your test will be, set that time aside for study. That way your brain will be used to working on that subject at that specific time and you'll have a better chance of recalling information.

Finally, it can be helpful to team up with others who are studying for the same test. Your actual studying should be done in as isolated an environment as possible, but the work of organizing the information and setting up the study plan can be divided up. In between study sessions, you can discuss with your teammates the concepts that you're all studying and quiz each other on the details. Just be sure that your teammates are as serious about the test as you are. If you find that your study time is being replaced with social time, you might need to find a new team.



Copyright © Mometrix Media. You have been licensed one copy of this document for personal use only. Any other reproduction or redistribution is strictly prohibited. All rights reserved.
This content is provided for test preparation purposes only and does not imply an endorsement by Mometrix of any particular political, scientific, or religious point of view.

# Secret Key #2 – Make Your Studying Count

You're devoting a lot of time and effort to preparing for this test, so you want to be absolutely certain it will pay off. This means doing more than just reading the content and hoping you can remember it on test day. It's important to make every minute of study count. There are two main areas you can focus on to make your studying count.

## Retention

It doesn't matter how much time you study if you can't remember the material. You need to make sure you are retaining the concepts. To check your retention of the information you're learning, try recalling it at later times with minimal prompting. Try carrying around flashcards and glance at one or two from time to time or ask a friend who's also studying for the test to quiz you.

To enhance your retention, look for ways to put the information into practice so that you can apply it rather than simply recalling it. If you're using the information in practical ways, it will be much easier to remember. Similarly, it helps to solidify a concept in your mind if you're not only reading it to yourself but also explaining it to someone else. Ask a friend to let you teach them about a concept you're a little shaky on (or speak aloud to an imaginary audience if necessary). As you try to summarize, define, give examples, and answer your friend's questions, you'll understand the concepts better and they will stay with you longer. Finally, step back for a big picture view and ask yourself how each piece of information fits with the whole subject. When you link the different concepts together and see them working together as a whole, it's easier to remember the individual components.

Finally, practice showing your work on any multi-step problems, even if you're just studying. Writing out each step you take to solve a problem will help solidify the process in your mind, and you'll be more likely to remember it during the test.

## Modality

*Modality* simply refers to the means or method by which you study. Choosing a study modality that fits your own individual learning style is crucial. No two people learn best in exactly the same way, so it's important to know your strengths and use them to your advantage.

For example, if you learn best by visualization, focus on visualizing a concept in your mind and draw an image or a diagram. Try color-coding your notes, illustrating them, or creating symbols that will trigger your mind to recall a learned concept. If you learn best by hearing or discussing information, find a study partner who learns the same way or read aloud to yourself. Think about how to put the information in your own words. Imagine that you are giving a lecture on the topic and record yourself so you can listen to it later.

For any learning style, flashcards can be helpful. Organize the information so you can take advantage of spare moments to review. Underline key words or phrases. Use different colors for different categories. Mnemonic devices (such as creating a short list in which every item starts with the same letter) can also help with retention. Find what works best for you and use it to store the information in your mind most effectively and easily.



Copyright © Mometrix Media. You have been licensed one copy of this document for personal use only. Any other reproduction or redistribution is strictly prohibited. All rights reserved.
This content is provided for test preparation purposes only and does not imply an endorsement by Mometrix of any particular political, scientific, or religious point of view.

# Secret Key #3 – Practice the Right Way

Your success on test day depends not only on how many hours you put into preparing, but also on whether you prepared the right way. It's good to check along the way to see if your studying is paying off. One of the most effective ways to do this is by taking practice tests to evaluate your progress. Practice tests are useful because they show exactly where you need to improve. Every time you take a practice test, pay special attention to these three groups of questions:

- The questions you got wrong
- The questions you had to guess on, even if you guessed right
- The questions you found difficult or slow to work through

This will show you exactly what your weak areas are, and where you need to devote more study time. Ask yourself why each of these questions gave you trouble. Was it because you didn't understand the material? Was it because you didn't remember the vocabulary? Do you need more repetitions on this type of question to build speed and confidence? Dig into those questions and figure out how you can strengthen your weak areas as you go back to review the material.

Additionally, many practice tests have a section explaining the answer choices. It can be tempting to read the explanation and think that you now have a good understanding of the concept. However, an explanation likely only covers part of the question's broader context. Even if the explanation makes perfect sense, **go back and investigate** every concept related to the question until you're positive you have a thorough understanding.

As you go along, keep in mind that the practice test is just that: practice. Memorizing these questions and answers will not be very helpful on the actual test because it is unlikely to have any of the same exact questions. If you only know the right answers to the sample questions, you won't be prepared for the real thing. **Study the concepts** until you understand them fully, and then you'll be able to answer any question that shows up on the test.

It's important to wait on the practice tests until you're ready. If you take a test on your first day of study, you may be overwhelmed by the amount of material covered and how much you need to learn. Work up to it gradually.

On test day, you'll need to be prepared for answering questions, managing your time, and using the test-taking strategies you've learned. It's a lot to balance, like a mental marathon that will have a big impact on your future. Like training for a marathon, you'll need to start slowly and work your way up. When test day arrives, you'll be ready.

Start with the strategies you've read in the first two Secret Keys—plan your course and study in the way that works best for you. If you have time, consider using multiple study resources to get different approaches to the same concepts. It can be helpful to see difficult concepts from more than one angle. Then find a good source for practice tests. Many times, the test website will suggest potential study resources or provide sample tests.



Copyright © Mometrix Media. You have been licensed one copy of this document for personal use only. Any other reproduction or redistribution is strictly prohibited. All rights reserved.
This content is provided for test preparation purposes only and does not imply an endorsement by Mometrix of any particular political, scientific, or religious point of view.

## Practice Test Strategy

If you're able to find at least three practice tests, we recommend this strategy:

### UNTIMED AND OPEN-BOOK PRACTICE

Take the first test with no time constraints and with your notes and study guide handy. Take your time and focus on applying the strategies you've learned.

### TIMED AND OPEN-BOOK PRACTICE

Take the second practice test open-book as well, but set a timer and practice pacing yourself to finish in time.

### TIMED AND CLOSED-BOOK PRACTICE

Take any other practice tests as if it were test day. Set a timer and put away your study materials. Sit at a table or desk in a quiet room, imagine yourself at the testing center, and answer questions as quickly and accurately as possible.

Keep repeating timed and closed-book tests on a regular basis until you run out of practice tests or it's time for the actual test. Your mind will be ready for the schedule and stress of test day, and you'll be able to focus on recalling the material you've learned.



Copyright © Mometrix Media. You have been licensed one copy of this document for personal use only. Any other reproduction or redistribution is strictly prohibited. All rights reserved.
This content is provided for test preparation purposes only and does not imply an endorsement by Mometrix of any particular political, scientific, or religious point of view.

# Secret Key #4 – Pace Yourself

Once you're fully prepared for the material on the test, your biggest challenge on test day will be managing your time. Just knowing that the clock is ticking can make you panic even if you have plenty of time left. Work on pacing yourself so you can build confidence against the time constraints of the exam. Pacing is a difficult skill to master, especially in a high-pressure environment, so **practice is vital**.

Set time expectations for your pace based on how much time is available. For example, if a section has 60 questions and the time limit is 30 minutes, you know you have to average 30 seconds or less per question in order to answer them all. Although 30 seconds is the hard limit, set 25 seconds per question as your goal, so you reserve extra time to spend on harder questions. When you budget extra time for the harder questions, you no longer have any reason to stress when those questions take longer to answer.

Don't let this time expectation distract you from working through the test at a calm, steady pace, but keep it in mind so you don't spend too much time on any one question. Recognize that taking extra time on one question you don't understand may keep you from answering two that you do understand later in the test. If your time limit for a question is up and you're still not sure of the answer, mark it and move on, and come back to it later if the time and the test format allow. If the testing format doesn't allow you to return to earlier questions, just make an educated guess; then put it out of your mind and move on.

On the easier questions, be careful not to rush. It may seem wise to hurry through them so you have more time for the challenging ones, but it's not worth missing one if you know the concept and just didn't take the time to read the question fully. Work efficiently but make sure you understand the question and have looked at all of the answer choices, since more than one may seem right at first.

Even if you're paying attention to the time, you may find yourself a little behind at some point. You should speed up to get back on track, but do so wisely. Don't panic; just take a few seconds less on each question until you're caught up. Don't guess without thinking, but do look through the answer choices and eliminate any you know are wrong. If you can get down to two choices, it is often worthwhile to guess from those. Once you've chosen an answer, move on and don't dwell on any that you skipped or had to hurry through. If a question was taking too long, chances are it was one of the harder ones, so you weren't as likely to get it right anyway.

On the other hand, if you find yourself getting ahead of schedule, it may be beneficial to slow down a little. The more quickly you work, the more likely you are to make a careless mistake that will affect your score. You've budgeted time for each question, so don't be afraid to spend that time. Practice an efficient but careful pace to get the most out of the time you have.



Copyright © Mometrix Media. You have been licensed one copy of this document for personal use only. Any other reproduction or redistribution is strictly prohibited. All rights reserved.
This content is provided for test preparation purposes only and does not imply an endorsement by Mometrix of any particular political, scientific, or religious point of view.

# Secret Key #5 – Have a Plan for Guessing

When you're taking the test, you may find yourself stuck on a question. Some of the answer choices seem better than others, but you don't see the one answer choice that is obviously correct. What do you do?

The scenario described above is very common, yet most test takers have not effectively prepared for it. Developing and practicing a plan for guessing may be one of the single most effective uses of your time as you get ready for the exam.

In developing your plan for guessing, there are three questions to address:

- When should you start the guessing process?
- How should you narrow down the choices?
- Which answer should you choose?

## When to Start the Guessing Process

Unless your plan for guessing is to select C every time (which, despite its merits, is not what we recommend), you need to leave yourself enough time to apply your answer elimination strategies. Since you have a limited amount of time for each question, that means that if you're going to give yourself the best shot at guessing correctly, you have to decide quickly whether or not you will guess.

Of course, the best-case scenario is that you don't have to guess at all, so first, see if you can answer the question based on your knowledge of the subject and basic reasoning skills. Focus on the key words in the question and try to jog your memory of related topics. Give yourself a chance to bring the knowledge to mind, but once you realize that you don't have (or you can't access) the knowledge you need to answer the question, it's time to start the guessing process.

It's almost always better to start the guessing process too early than too late. It only takes a few seconds to remember something and answer the question from knowledge. Carefully eliminating wrong answer choices takes longer. Plus, going through the process of eliminating answer choices can actually help jog your memory.

**Summary**: Start the guessing process as soon as you decide that you can't answer the question based on your knowledge.



Copyright © Mometrix Media. You have been licensed one copy of this document for personal use only. Any other reproduction or redistribution is strictly prohibited. All rights reserved.
This content is provided for test preparation purposes only and does not imply an endorsement by Mometrix of any particular political, scientific, or religious point of view.

## How to Narrow Down the Choices

The next chapter in this book (**Test-Taking Strategies**) includes a wide range of strategies for how to approach questions and how to look for answer choices to eliminate. You will definitely want to read those carefully, practice them, and figure out which ones work best for you. Here though, we're going to address a mindset rather than a particular strategy.

Your odds of guessing an answer correctly depend on how many options you are choosing from.

| Number of options left | 5 | 4 | 3 | 2 | 1 |
|---|---|---|---|---|---|
| Odds of guessing correctly | 20% | 25% | 33% | 50% | 100% |

You can see from this chart just how valuable it is to be able to eliminate incorrect answers and make an educated guess, but there are two things that many test takers do that cause them to miss out on the benefits of guessing:

- Accidentally eliminating the correct answer
- Selecting an answer based on an impression

We'll look at the first one here, and the second one in the next section.

To avoid accidentally eliminating the correct answer, we recommend a thought exercise called **the $5 challenge**. In this challenge, you only eliminate an answer choice from contention if you are willing to bet $5 on it being wrong. Why $5? Five dollars is a small but not insignificant amount of money. It's an amount you could afford to lose but wouldn't want to throw away. And while losing $5 once might not hurt too much, doing it twenty times will set you back $100. In the same way, each small decision you make—eliminating a choice here, guessing on a question there—won't by itself impact your score very much, but when you put them all together, they can make a big difference. By holding each answer choice elimination decision to a higher standard, you can reduce the risk of accidentally eliminating the correct answer.

The $5 challenge can also be applied in a positive sense: If you are willing to bet $5 that an answer choice *is* correct, go ahead and mark it as correct.

**Summary**: Only eliminate an answer choice if you are willing to bet $5 that it is wrong.



Copyright © Mometrix Media. You have been licensed one copy of this document for personal use only. Any other reproduction or redistribution is strictly prohibited. All rights reserved.
This content is provided for test preparation purposes only and does not imply an endorsement by Mometrix of any particular political, scientific, or religious point of view.

# Which Answer to Choose

You're taking the test. You've run into a hard question and decided you'll have to guess. You've eliminated all the answer choices you're willing to bet $5 on. Now you have to pick an answer. Why do we even need to talk about this? Why can't you just pick whichever one you feel like when the time comes?

The answer to these questions is that if you don't come into the test with a plan, you'll rely on your impression to select an answer choice, and if you do that, you risk falling into a trap. The test writers know that everyone who takes their test will be guessing on some of the questions, so they intentionally write wrong answer choices to seem plausible. You still have to pick an answer though, and if the wrong answer choices are designed to look right, how can you ever be sure that you're not falling for their trap? The best solution we've found to this dilemma is to take the decision out of your hands entirely. Here is the process we recommend:

**Once you've eliminated any choices that you are confident (willing to bet $5) are wrong, select the first remaining choice as your answer.**

Whether you choose to select the first remaining choice, the second, or the last, the important thing is that you use some preselected standard. Using this approach guarantees that you will not be enticed into selecting an answer choice that looks right, because you are not basing your decision on how the answer choices look.

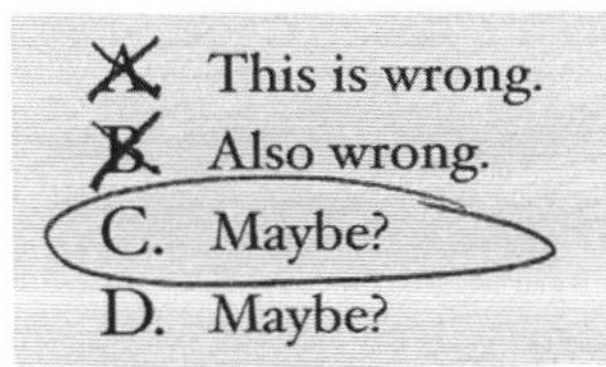


This is not meant to make you question your knowledge. Instead, it is to help you recognize the difference between your knowledge and your impressions. There's a huge difference between thinking an answer is right because of what you know, and thinking an answer is right because it looks or sounds like it should be right.

**Summary**: To ensure that your selection is appropriately random, make a predetermined selection from among all answer choices you have not eliminated.



Copyright © Mometrix Media. You have been licensed one copy of this document for personal use only. Any other reproduction or redistribution is strictly prohibited. All rights reserved.
This content is provided for test preparation purposes only and does not imply an endorsement by Mometrix of any particular political, scientific, or religious point of view.

# Test-Taking Strategies

This section contains a list of test-taking strategies that you may find helpful as you work through the test. By taking what you know and applying logical thought, you can maximize your chances of answering any question correctly!

It is very important to realize that every question is different and every person is different: no single strategy will work on every question, and no single strategy will work for every person. That's why we've included all of them here, so you can try them out and determine which ones work best for different types of questions and which ones work best for you.

## Question Strategies

### ⊘ Read Carefully

Read the question and the answer choices carefully. Don't miss the question because you misread the terms. You have plenty of time to read each question thoroughly and make sure you understand what is being asked. Yet a happy medium must be attained, so don't waste too much time. You must read carefully and efficiently.

### ⊘ Contextual Clues

Look for contextual clues. If the question includes a word you are not familiar with, look at the immediate context for some indication of what the word might mean. Contextual clues can often give you all the information you need to decipher the meaning of an unfamiliar word. Even if you can't determine the meaning, you may be able to narrow down the possibilities enough to make a solid guess at the answer to the question.

### ⊘ Prefixes

If you're having trouble with a word in the question or answer choices, try dissecting it. Take advantage of every clue that the word might include. Prefixes can be a huge help. Usually, they allow you to determine a basic meaning. *Pre-* means before, *post-* means after, *pro-* is positive, *de-* is negative. From prefixes, you can get an idea of the general meaning of the word and try to put it into context.

### ⊘ Hedge Words

Watch out for critical hedge words, such as *likely, may, can, often, almost, mostly, usually, generally, rarely,* and *sometimes.* Question writers insert these hedge phrases to cover every possibility. Often an answer choice will be wrong simply because it leaves no room for exception. Be on guard for answer choices that have definitive words such as *exactly* and *always.*

### ⊘ Switchback Words

Stay alert for *switchbacks.* These are the words and phrases frequently used to alert you to shifts in thought. The most common switchback words are *but, although,* and *however.* Others include *nevertheless, on the other hand, even though, while, in spite of, despite,* and *regardless of.* Switchback words are important to catch because they can change the direction of the question or an answer choice.



Copyright © Mometrix Media. You have been licensed one copy of this document for personal use only. Any other reproduction or redistribution is strictly prohibited. All rights reserved.
This content is provided for test preparation purposes only and does not imply an endorsement by Mometrix of any particular political, scientific, or religious point of view.

### ⊘ FACE VALUE

When in doubt, use common sense. Accept the situation in the problem at face value. Don't read too much into it. These problems will not require you to make wild assumptions. If you have to go beyond creativity and warp time or space in order to have an answer choice fit the question, then you should move on and consider the other answer choices. These are normal problems rooted in reality. The applicable relationship or explanation may not be readily apparent, but it is there for you to figure out. Use your common sense to interpret anything that isn't clear.

## Answer Choice Strategies

### ⊘ ANSWER SELECTION

The most thorough way to pick an answer choice is to identify and eliminate wrong answers until only one is left, then confirm it is the correct answer. Sometimes an answer choice may immediately seem right, but be careful. The test writers will usually put more than one reasonable answer choice on each question, so take a second to read all of them and make sure that the other choices are not equally obvious. As long as you have time left, it is better to read every answer choice than to pick the first one that looks right without checking the others.

### ⊘ ANSWER CHOICE FAMILIES

An answer choice family consists of two (in rare cases, three) answer choices that are very similar in construction and cannot all be true at the same time. If you see two answer choices that are direct opposites or parallels, one of them is usually the correct answer. For instance, if one answer choice says that quantity *x* increases and another either says that quantity *x* decreases (opposite) or says that quantity *y* increases (parallel), then those answer choices would fall into the same family. An answer choice that doesn't match the construction of the answer choice family is more likely to be incorrect. Most questions will not have answer choice families, but when they do appear, you should be prepared to recognize them.

### ⊘ ELIMINATE ANSWERS

Eliminate answer choices as soon as you realize they are wrong, but make sure you consider all possibilities. If you are eliminating answer choices and realize that the last one you are left with is also wrong, don't panic. Start over and consider each choice again. There may be something you missed the first time that you will realize on the second pass.

### ⊘ AVOID FACT TRAPS

Don't be distracted by an answer choice that is factually true but doesn't answer the question. You are looking for the choice that answers the question. Stay focused on what the question is asking for so you don't accidentally pick an answer that is true but incorrect. Always go back to the question and make sure the answer choice you've selected actually answers the question and is not merely a true statement.

### ⊘ EXTREME STATEMENTS

In general, you should avoid answers that put forth extreme actions as standard practice or proclaim controversial ideas as established fact. An answer choice that states the "process should be used in certain situations, if…" is much more likely to be correct than one that states the "process should be discontinued completely." The first is a calm rational statement and doesn't even make a definitive, uncompromising stance, using a hedge word *if* to provide wiggle room, whereas the second choice is far more extreme.



Copyright © Mometrix Media. You have been licensed one copy of this document for personal use only. Any other reproduction or redistribution is strictly prohibited. All rights reserved.
This content is provided for test preparation purposes only and does not imply an endorsement by Mometrix of any particular political, scientific, or religious point of view.

### ⊘ BENCHMARK

As you read through the answer choices and you come across one that seems to answer the question well, mentally select that answer choice. This is not your final answer, but it's the one that will help you evaluate the other answer choices. The one that you selected is your benchmark or standard for judging each of the other answer choices. Every other answer choice must be compared to your benchmark. That choice is correct until proven otherwise by another answer choice beating it. If you find a better answer, then that one becomes your new benchmark. Once you've decided that no other choice answers the question as well as your benchmark, you have your final answer.

### ⊘ PREDICT THE ANSWER

Before you even start looking at the answer choices, it is often best to try to predict the answer. When you come up with the answer on your own, it is easier to avoid distractions and traps because you will know exactly what to look for. The right answer choice is unlikely to be word-for-word what you came up with, but it should be a close match. Even if you are confident that you have the right answer, you should still take the time to read each option before moving on.

## General Strategies

### ⊘ TOUGH QUESTIONS

If you are stumped on a problem or it appears too hard or too difficult, don't waste time. Move on! Remember though, if you can quickly check for obviously incorrect answer choices, your chances of guessing correctly are greatly improved. Before you completely give up, at least try to knock out a couple of possible answers. Eliminate what you can and then guess at the remaining answer choices before moving on.

### ⊘ CHECK YOUR WORK

Since you will probably not know every term listed and the answer to every question, it is important that you get credit for the ones that you do know. Don't miss any questions through careless mistakes. If at all possible, try to take a second to look back over your answer selection and make sure you've selected the correct answer choice and haven't made a costly careless mistake (such as marking an answer choice that you didn't mean to mark). This quick double check should more than pay for itself in caught mistakes for the time it costs.

### ⊘ PACE YOURSELF

It's easy to be overwhelmed when you're looking at a page full of questions; your mind is confused and full of random thoughts, and the clock is ticking down faster than you would like. Calm down and maintain the pace that you have set for yourself. Especially as you get down to the last few minutes of the test, don't let the small numbers on the clock make you panic. As long as you are on track by monitoring your pace, you are guaranteed to have time for each question.

### ⊘ DON'T RUSH

It is very easy to make errors when you are in a hurry. Maintaining a fast pace in answering questions is pointless if it makes you miss questions that you would have gotten right otherwise. Test writers like to include distracting information and wrong answers that seem right. Taking a little extra time to avoid careless mistakes can make all the difference in your test score. Find a pace that allows you to be confident in the answers that you select.



Copyright © Mometrix Media. You have been licensed one copy of this document for personal use only. Any other reproduction or redistribution is strictly prohibited. All rights reserved.
This content is provided for test preparation purposes only and does not imply an endorsement by Mometrix of any particular political, scientific, or religious point of view.

### ⊘ Keep Moving

Panicking will not help you pass the test, so do your best to stay calm and keep moving. Taking deep breaths and going through the answer elimination steps you practiced can help to break through a stress barrier and keep your pace.

## Final Notes

The combination of a solid foundation of content knowledge and the confidence that comes from practicing your plan for applying that knowledge is the key to maximizing your performance on test day. As your foundation of content knowledge is built up and strengthened, you'll find that the strategies included in this chapter become more and more effective in helping you quickly sift through the distractions and traps of the test to isolate the correct answer.

Now that you're preparing to move forward into the test content chapters of this book, be sure to keep your goal in mind. As you read, think about how you will be able to apply this information on the test. If you've already seen sample questions for the test and you have an idea of the question format and style, try to come up with questions of your own that you can answer based on what you're reading. This will give you valuable practice applying your knowledge in the same ways you can expect to on test day.

**Good luck and good studying!**



Copyright © Mometrix Media. You have been licensed one copy of this document for personal use only. Any other reproduction or redistribution is strictly prohibited. All rights reserved.
This content is provided for test preparation purposes only and does not imply an endorsement by Mometrix of any particular political, scientific, or religious point of view.

Copyright © Mometrix Media. You have been licensed one copy of this document for personal use only. Any other reproduction or redistribution is strictly prohibited. All rights reserved.
This content is provided for test preparation purposes only and does not imply an endorsement by Mometrix of any particular political, scientific, or religious point of view.

# Reading

## Word Analysis and Vocabulary

### USING CONTEXT TO DETERMINE THE MEANINGS OF WORDS

Readers of all levels will encounter words that they have either never seen or that they have seen before but still don't know what it means. The best way to define a word in **context** is to look for nearby words that can assist in learning the meaning of the word.

#### *CONTEXT CLUES*

Context clues are hints about the meaning of a word. They are the words or phrases in the sentence or sentences before and after a new or unfamiliar word. Context clues give the reader an idea about what a word means. A context clue may also contain words that help define the new word or an example of what the new word means. Using context clues to figure out meaning can be helpful when learning a new set of vocabulary words or reading a difficult text. The dictionary definition of a word can always be looked up to double-check intended meaning.

#### *SUBSTITUTION TO FIND MEANING*

One way to find out if you have figured out the correct meaning of a new word is to **substitute** the meaning for the word. Using the example for *reluctant*, if the reader substituted in "not willing," the sentence would read

> Sam was "not willing" to be in the play, so he told the director that he was too busy to rehearse and didn't go to tryouts. He felt to shy to get up on a stage.

<u>EXAMPLE</u>

Using context clues, determine the meaning of the word *staggered* in the following sentence:

> As soon as he heard his Father's voice, he jumped up from his seat to open the door, but, as he did so, he *staggered* and fell headlong to the floor.

In the example, the word *staggered* refers to the action the character was taking before he "fell headlong to the floor". The reader knows that the character was on his feet, but that he did not have his balance. This information helps the reader decide that the word *staggered* means to move unsteadily.

#### *SYNONYMS AND ANTONYMS*

When you understand how words relate to each other, you will discover more in a passage. This is explained by understanding **synonyms**, which are words that mean the same thing, and **antonyms**, which are words that mean the opposite of one another. As an example, *dry* and *arid* are synonyms, and *dry* and *wet* are antonyms.

**Review Video: <u>Synonyms and Antonyms</u>**
Visit mometrix.com/academy and enter code: 105612



Copyright © Mometrix Media. You have been licensed one copy of this document for personal use only. Any other reproduction or redistribution is strictly prohibited. All rights reserved.
This content is provided for test preparation purposes only and does not imply an endorsement by Mometrix of any particular political, scientific, or religious point of view.

### EXAMPLE

Read the following sentences and determine the meaning of the word *reluctant* based on context clues:

> Sam was *reluctant* to be in the play, so he told the director that he was too busy to rehearse and didn't go to tryouts. He felt too shy to get up on a stage.

In this example sentence, the words "too busy" show that Sam made an excuse about why he couldn't be in the school play. The sentence also says that he "didn't go to tryouts." The second example sentence has other clues. It says, "He felt too shy to get up on stage." These clues give the reader hints about what the word *reluctant* means. It means "not willing."

## MULTIPLE-MEANING WORDS

A multiple-meaning word has different definitions, depending on the contextual use of the word. A multiple-meaning word is also called a **homonym**. A homonym is defined as a word that has more than one meaning, but is spelled and pronounced the same for all of them. For example, look at the word *leaves* in the following two sentences:

- Michelle *leaves* the building at 5 o'clock every day.
- The *leaves* fell off the oak tree in September.

In the first sentence, *leaves* means exits. In the second sentence, *leaves* refers to parts of a tree. By looking at the rest of each sentence, the reader can understand which definition of the multiple-meaning word the author is referring to.

## SIMILAR WORDS

**Homophones** are words that are pronounced the same, but may be spelled differently. An example of two homophones would be *heir* (someone due to inherit an estate) and *air* (the invisible substance people breathe).

**Homographs** are words that are spelled the same, but may be pronounced differently. An example of a homograph is the word *row*, which is pronounced one way when used to mean a horizontal grouping and is pronounced another way when used to mean an argument.

## ROOT WORDS, PREFIXES, AND SUFFIXES

A **root word** is the base word, before an affix, in the form of a prefix, infix, or suffix, is added onto it. Many affixes in the English language come from Latin or Greek origins. A **prefix** is added onto the beginning of a root word, an **infix** is added into the middle, and a **suffix** is added onto the end of a root word. By looking at the meaning of a root word and the meaning of any affixes added to it, the reader can figure out the approximate meaning of the word. For example, the root word 'like' means to enjoy and the prefix 'dis-' means not. The reader can therefore understand that the full word 'dislike' means to not enjoy.

A reader can use root words and affixes to figure out the general meaning of an unknown word. Knowing root words and affixes is helpful on tests where analogies are made using unfamiliar words. By figuring out the general meaning of a new word, a tester can figure out the general relationship presented between two words.



Copyright © Mometrix Media. You have been licensed one copy of this document for personal use only. Any other reproduction or redistribution is strictly prohibited. All rights reserved.
This content is provided for test preparation purposes only and does not imply an endorsement by Mometrix of any particular political, scientific, or religious point of view.

### Common Greek Root Words

| Root | Meaning | Example |
|---|---|---|
| auto | self | automobile (a self-propelled vehicle) |
| geo | earth or ground | geography (study of the earth) |
| photo | light | photon (a small particle of light) |

### Common Prefixes

| Prefix | Meaning | Example |
|---|---|---|
| trans- | across, through, or change | translate (to write or say in a different language) |
| super- | over or greater than | superhuman (greater than a regular human) |
| sub- | under | submerge (to sink below the surface) |

### Common Suffixes

| Suffix | Meaning | Example |
|---|---|---|
| -ive | cause to, tend to, or doing | creative (a person who tends to make new things or think of new ideas) |
| -logy | study of | biology (study of life) |
| -ful | full of | wonderful (full of wonder) |

### Example

Using knowledge of affixes, determine meaning of the word *attentive* in the following sentence

Jorge was a very *attentive* student in Social Studies class, but in Math, he often lost focus.

The word *attentive* contains the suffix "-ive," which means cause to, tend to, or doing. Readers may recognize the beginning of the word, "attent" as the same beginning as the word "attention." Based on the context, the reader can infer that this word means Jorge tends to pay attention in class, especially because of the contrast shown by the second half of the sentence.

## Synonyms and Antonyms

When you understand how words relate to each other, you will discover more in a passage. This is explained by understanding **synonyms** (words that mean the same thing) and **antonyms** (words that mean the opposite of one another). As an example, *dry* and *arid* are synonyms, and *dry* and *wet* are antonyms.



Copyright © Mometrix Media. You have been licensed one copy of this document for personal use only. Any other reproduction or redistribution is strictly prohibited. All rights reserved.
This content is provided for test preparation purposes only and does not imply an endorsement by Mometrix of any particular political, scientific, or religious point of view.

### *Example*

Read the following sentences and determine the meaning of the word *reluctant* based on context clues:

> Sam was *reluctant* to be in the play, so he told the director that he was too busy to rehearse and didn't go to tryouts. He felt too shy to get up on a stage.

In this example sentence, the words "too busy" show that Sam made an excuse about why he couldn't be in the school play. The sentence also says that he "didn't go to tryouts." The second example sentence has other clues. It says, "He felt too shy to get up on stage." These clues give the reader hints about what the word *reluctant* means. It means "not willing."

### Dictionary

A print or digital dictionary can be used to find out many things about a word. A dictionary will show the correct pronunciation of a word, provide its meaning, and identify what part of speech the word is. It will also tell how the word was derived—that is, what words it came from originally. A dictionary will have a **pronunciation guide** for each word that shows how to sound it out and where its syllables start and end. It will use symbols to indicate sounds, and will also use sample sounds (the "a" in "bad," for instance). A dictionary lists all of the meanings of a word and the parts of speech the word can be used as.

> **example** \ ig-ˈzam-pəl\ noun
> 1. something that shows what a group of things is like
> 2. a model that should be either copied or avoided
> 3. a punishment meant to serve as a warning to others

### *Example:*

Julia used her dictionary to check the various meanings of the word *clear*. She found this entry:

> **clear** (klîr) adjective
> 1. obvious.
> 2. easily seen through
> 3. free from flaw or blemish
> 4. free from guilt; untroubled
> 5. out of the way
> 6. to tidy *v*
> 7. to free *v*
> 8. to earn *v*

Identify which definition of *clear* is used in the following sentence:

> Janet stood *clear* of the crowd pushing to get through the door.

The correct answer is meaning 5: "out of the way." If you substitute that definition for the word, the sentence makes sense. Meanings 1, 2, 3, and 4 do not fit with the context of the sentence. Meanings 6, 7, and 8 are verbs and "clear" as it is used in the sample is an adjective. When considering which



Copyright © Mometrix Media. You have been licensed one copy of this document for personal use only. Any other reproduction or redistribution is strictly prohibited. All rights reserved.
This content is provided for test preparation purposes only and does not imply an endorsement by Mometrix of any particular political, scientific, or religious point of view.

meaning is being used, always check for context clues in the sentence or in the sentences before or after the sentence in which the word is used.

### THESAURUS

A thesaurus is a reference book that gives **synonyms** of words. It is different from a dictionary because a thesaurus does not give definitions. A thesaurus can be helpful in finding the meaning of an unfamiliar word when reading. If the meaning of a synonym is known, then the meaning of the unfamiliar word will be known. Another time in which a thesaurus can be helpful is when writing. Using a thesaurus helps authors to vary their word choice.

### GLOSSARY

A glossary is a **list of terms and their definitions** that can be found **at the back** of certain types of books, such as textbooks or reference books. A glossary does not have the definitions of all words, like a dictionary, but instead gives the definitions of the important terms within that particular book which are either uncommon or newly introduced. One may use a glossary when reading a book about economics or a chapter in a science textbook, for example, to define some of the technical terms within the text.

## Literal and Figurative Language

### LITERAL AND FIGURATIVE LANGUAGE

Many types of text use both **literal language**, which means just what it says, and **figurative language**, which means something more than the literal words being used. Figurative language is a literary device that allows the author to expand reality in a vivid way. When an author uses figurative language, she connects things in an exaggerated way in order to create a memorable image, which helps to describe a situation in a new way for the reader.

**Review Video: Figurative Language**
Visit mometrix.com/academy and enter code: 584902

### IMAGERY

Imagery is the use of **descriptive language** to add life or feeling to a work of literature. Many authors add literary and sound devices to create vivid pictures in the minds of their readers. Most of the time, imagery is thought to be one of the best ways to help readers fully understand and remember a work.

The most common forms of imagery are those that appeal to the sense of sight and sound. Imagery that appeals to the sense of sight, or **visual imagery**, helps the reader picture an event in their mind, usually by including specific details in the text that are not strictly necessary for the purpose of the story, but allow the reader to more easily envision the scene. Some common forms of figurative language that help create visual imagery include.

#### *METAPHOR*

- Puts one idea in place of another to draw a parallel between the two ideas.
- For example, an author might write "Her room was a pigsty," to compare a person's bedroom to a dirty spot where pigs sleep.

#### *SIMILE*

- Shows similarity between two ideas or objects, using the words "**like**" or "**as**"



Copyright © Mometrix Media. You have been licensed one copy of this document for personal use only. Any other reproduction or redistribution is strictly prohibited. All rights reserved.
This content is provided for test preparation purposes only and does not imply an endorsement by Mometrix of any particular political, scientific, or religious point of view.

- For example, an author might write "The princess is as beautiful as a rose" to compare the appearance of a woman to a beautiful flower.

#### *Symbolism*

- Using one object to stand for something else.
- For example, an author may include a flag flying high throughout a story to show pride in the characters' country and to represent the idea of patriotism.

#### *Hyperbole*

- An extreme exaggeration of an idea.
- For example, a character might say "I'm starving to death!" to show that they are really hungry. Most of the time a character who says this is not literally going to die from hunger, they are just ready for a snack.

#### *Irony*

- Uses sarcasm or humor (usually with an emphasis on the opposite) to show difference from literal meaning.
- For example, if a character says "Well today must be my lucky day!" after they left their homework on the kitchen table, they are being ironic. The irony used here helps show that it is definitely *not* the character's lucky day.

#### *Personification*

- Gives life or human characteristics to an inanimate object
- For example, if an author writes "The trees whispered to each other across the wide blue sky," they are using personification to help the reader imagine the scene. Trees are not human beings, so they do not whisper, but the image created in the reader stands out more than a literal description would.

#### *Example*

Based on current knowledge, identify whether metaphor, simile, or hyperbole is used in this sentence:

> The chiming bell was a beacon of hope for the downtrodden villagers.

A metaphor is used in this sentence to draw a parallel between "the chiming bell" and "a beacon of hope." The bell is being compared to something else in the sentence, which indicates the use of metaphor or simile, but the reader knows that the sentence does not contain a simile, because the words **like** and **as** are not used to show the comparison. The sentence also does not contain an exaggeration of facts, so the reader can see that hyperbole is not used.

### Sound Devices

Sound devices allow authors to add another level to their texts by tapping into the spoken part of language. Imagery that appeals to the sense of hearing, or **auditory imagery**. Authors may use many sound devices to create meaning and help readers understand them better, including

#### *Onomatopoeia*

- Appeals to the reader's sense of hearing by using words that copy the noises objects or people make, like sound effects.
- For example, an author might write "The soccer ball whooshed across the field into the goalie's net, scoring the winning point!" The word "whooshed" is an onomatopoeia because it mimics the sound of air moving quickly. Because the writer chose to include an onomatopoeia, the reader is able to better picture the action in the sentence.



Copyright © Mometrix Media. You have been licensed one copy of this document for personal use only. Any other reproduction or redistribution is strictly prohibited. All rights reserved.
This content is provided for test preparation purposes only and does not imply an endorsement by Mometrix of any particular political, scientific, or religious point of view.

# Elements of Story

## Setting

The setting is where a story **takes place**. The setting of a story may stay the same for the entire story, or change as events in the story unfold. For example, an entire story may take place in one room, or on the other end, a story could cross continents as the reader follows the characters along on a trail of events. Every story has to take place somewhere. The setting of story is described by the author in terms of what it looks like, how the character feels, and anything that is happening at that location at the time. For example, a character may be caught on a doorstep on a cold, rainy day. The character may feel frustrated as he shivers in the doorway, waiting for the heavy rain to let up a bit.

### *Example*

When listing ways that a story set in the city has a different backdrop from a story set in the countryside, answers will vary based on current knowledge of common characteristics for each setting. A story set in a city may be different from a story set in the countryside based on the following factors:

- Number of passersby: many people on a sidewalk vs. no other people around
- Background noise: car horns vs. bird calls
- Types of surroundings: tall buildings vs. fields of corn
- Types of transportation: subways and taxis vs. horses and farm trucks
- Daily activities being carried out: sitting at a desk in a skyscraper vs. plowing fields for planting
- Type of attire: a business suit vs. dirty jeans and boots

### *Shaping a Character with Setting or Plot*

The setting of a story shapes character because it helps to define the situation that a character finds herself in. A character is limited to the setting of a story. For example, if a story takes place in a cold environment filled with snow and ice, this is certain to impact what actions a character can and will take. Frequently, the setting changes the way characters behave based on time. For example, the character of a woman who is a single mother in 1920 would be seen and behave very differently than a single mother in 2020.

#### Example

Read the excerpt and determine how the setting influences the character in this excerpt.

> She had swum too far out. The waves were higher than she thought. She was struggling hard to get to shore. She wondered if she would make it. She thought of her childhood. Had she been right to run away from home, she wondered? Just then, a lifeguard grabbed her and helped her to shore.

The setting of the ocean and the high waves creates a conflict in the character. She is worried. She thinks about her childhood and her parents. She doesn't know if she will make it to shore. This is how the setting affects the character in this excerpt. Without the high waves and the struggle, she would not become so worried and start to think about her past. She probably would not have questioned herself. This is an example of how a setting influences a character. If the waves had not been high, there probably would not have been a struggle or any self-searching of the swimmer's past.



Copyright © Mometrix Media. You have been licensed one copy of this document for personal use only. Any other reproduction or redistribution is strictly prohibited. All rights reserved.
This content is provided for test preparation purposes only and does not imply an endorsement by Mometrix of any particular political, scientific, or religious point of view.

### *Historical and Cultural Setting*

Historical context influences literature in a number of ways. The style of the author's writing can be impacted by the historical period during which it was written (e.g., Dickens wrote at a time when authors were paid by the word; this is why his novels are so long). Obviously, the setting of the book includes its historical context. In addition, dialect may be a function of the historical period of the book. When a reader understands the historical context of a particular book, he or she can have a deeper understanding of the novel. Knowing about the time period during which the author wrote, as well as the time period discussed in the novel, helps the reader understand some of the author's choices, including character motivations.

### *Patterns Related to Settings*

The setting of a story can allow the reader to draw on personal experience about where the story takes place. If a story takes place on a farm, the reader will likely picture a rural, peaceful setting, which may go along with (or be in contrast to) the actual plot of the story. For example, a reader would not expect a scary story to occur on a farm on a sunny day. Conversely, a reader may view a dark subway as a dangerous place, while the plot of a story set there may be based on a very calm series of events. When an author is crafting a story, they need to consider what the audience may already think about a particular setting in order to properly present the events of a story for greatest impact.

## Style and Voice

Style and voice play an important role in the development of a story. The reader's impression of a story can vary based on the style and voice used by the author. **Style** refers to the way an author uses words, phrases, and sentence structure. The style of the text can change depending on whether the author uses short, choppy sentences, long, elaborate sentences, formal language, or informal language. **Voice** refers to the characteristics of a text that show the author's personality and distinguish the author from other writers. An author's voice may be recognized through the way they use words or the way they organize and present their thoughts. Voice is specific to each writer, and it can be as specific and unique as personality.

## Plot

The term **plot** refers to the series of events that take place in a story. The events in a story may take place in one location or many, in a short amount of time or over many years. A story always has to start somewhere, and the first event in a story signals the beginning of the plot. Stories may vary in length from half a page to novel-length, but they all follow a progression of events that the author winds together to form the plot. The characters and events in the story determine what the plot



Copyright © Mometrix Media. You have been licensed one copy of this document for personal use only. Any other reproduction or redistribution is strictly prohibited. All rights reserved.
This content is provided for test preparation purposes only and does not imply an endorsement by Mometrix of any particular political, scientific, or religious point of view.

will be. Readers may find a **plot line** useful as they try to put the events in the text in order and determine the relationships between events.

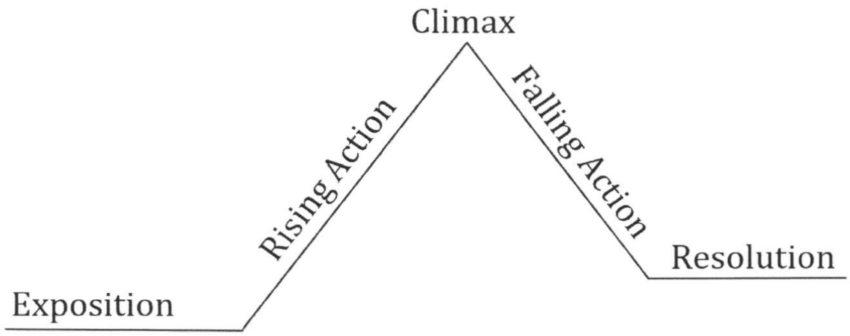


**Review Video: Plot Line**
Visit mometrix.com/academy and enter code: 944011

Every plot will begin with **exposition**, which introduces the characters and the setting of the story. The plot will continue to develop as new ideas and events centered on the main conflict in the story are revealed, which is called the **rising action**. The action in the story will rise until a **climax** is reached within the conflict. The climax can also be referred to as the turning point in the story, since the climax is where each character makes an important decision. After the climax, the action starts to wind down during the **falling action**. At this point, the characters begin to follow the paths they chose in during climax. The events of the story reach **resolution** in some way by the end of the story. Some conflicts are left open-ended, so that the reader is left to decide what really happened at the end of the story. Keep in mind that not all resolutions are happy or peaceful.

### *Example*

Read the following plot and determine what the missing event is in the plot sequence:

> Sarita went to the store to buy eggs for her mother. She bought the eggs and got back on her bicycle to bring the eggs home. Her mother was angry that the eggs were all broken.

The reader has to guess based on the plot sequence what happened between events. The reader knows that Sarita got on her bicycle to go home. The reader also knows that the eggs were broken when she arrived at the house. Based on the context, the reader can assume that Sarita fell off her bicycle or dropped the eggs on the way home, causing them to all be broken when she arrived. The reader can assume that Sarita would have noticed if the eggs were already broken in the store. Plot often follows a logical sequence of events, but sometimes it is difficult to decide what actually happened between two events. In the example, the reader can logically assume that the eggs were broken on the way home.

### *Conflict*

Conflict creates the basis for the plot of a story. A conflict may be between characters, a character and their own mind, or an outside influence. The main point of a conflict is that there is a problem that needs to be resolved. The problem may be a disagreement or an obstacle that has arisen and needs to be overcome.

An important part of analyzing the plot of a passage is identifying the **main conflict**. There will likely be many smaller conflicts in the story, but there will be one main problem that influences the characters and events. To identify the main conflict, first look at who the main character is. Now ask



Copyright © Mometrix Media. You have been licensed one copy of this document for personal use only. Any other reproduction or redistribution is strictly prohibited. All rights reserved.
This content is provided for test preparation purposes only and does not imply an endorsement by Mometrix of any particular political, scientific, or religious point of view.

yourself what they want. They may want to something to happen or not happen, another character to do or not do something, or to confront or avoid a problem, among other things. Once you know what they want, now ask yourself what is standing in the character's way. It may be a person, an event, or something less tangible like the passing of time. Combining what the main character wants and why they do not currently have leaves the reader with a summary of the main conflict.

**Review Video: Conflict**
Visit mometrix.com/academy and enter code: 559550

#### Example

Read the following sentence and explain the main conflict between the two characters:

> Joe stared angrily at Jamie's retreating back as Jamie raced away down the field with Joe's soccer ball.

The main conflict in the sentence is that Jamie has Joe's soccer ball. There may be additional conflicts between the two characters, but none are evident from the evidence shown in the sentence. In any story, a conflict may be minor and only affect part of the story, or be the main focus, taking an entire story to solve a conflict between characters. In the context of the sentence, it is not clear whether or not the entire story will revolve around Jamie taking Joe's soccer ball.

### *Resolution*

The term **resolution** usually indicates the result of a conflict in a story. Conflict between characters, within a character, or against an external element is necessary in order to have a plot for a story. Without conflict, no events would occur to form the story. A conflict will come to a climax, and then conclude in some way. The resolution of a problem may be open-ended, end tragically, or end in a way that is good for everyone involved. The problem resolution typically occurs near the end of a story, after the climax has happened. A problem may be resolved by the characters involved within the conflict or by an external event; an upcoming resolution may be foreshadowed in the text, or may be completely unexpected by the reader. If the resolution is completely unexpected, it is considered to be a **twist** in the story.

### *Effect of Plot on a Story's Characters*

The plot of a story unfolds as each event follows another, shaping the characters as they react to the various events that occur. Some characters are able to resolve their problems by the end of the story, while some characters fail to overcome their predicaments. As characters respond to the events around them, they reveal more and more about their personalities. Some grow and some do not. The reader can use the events of the plot to interpret the meaning of the story and understand its characters.

#### Example

Read the excerpt and explain how finding the chest affects Marta.

> The map said this was the spot. Marta held her breath. Her fists were clenched into two tight balls. She lifted the shovel and scooped more sand out of the hole. There it was; she had found the chest with the diamonds. She opened the top. She would never need to work again. She smiled. It was really happening.

The event affects Marta by making her happy. The reader gets several clues that she is anxiously waiting ("Marta held her breath" and "her fists were clenched"), and that she is happy with what she found ("She smiled"). Events can cause characters to have all kinds of feelings. Here, something



Copyright © Mometrix Media. You have been licensed one copy of this document for personal use only. Any other reproduction or redistribution is strictly prohibited. All rights reserved.
This content is provided for test preparation purposes only and does not imply an endorsement by Mometrix of any particular political, scientific, or religious point of view.

wonderful happened. However, events in stories are not always quite so happy. For instance, if a robber had suddenly seen Marta and the chest, he might have stolen the chest. That event would have had a very different effect on her. Readers need to pay attention to how characters are reacting to events, whether they are simply hinted at or stated in the story. In this way a reader will learn what characters are like.

## CHARACTERS

### *CHARACTER TRAIT*

The traits of a character may include how they act and physical characteristics; a character trait is a behavior or physical characteristic that is unique to a specific character. For example, a character may be outgoing, which means he or she likes to talk a lot, or they may have bright red hair. These are both character traits.

An author uses character traits to describe a character in a story and help the reader to learn more about how the character acts and what they look like. By comparing the character traits in a story, the reader can see similarities and differences between characters. The author includes character traits to help the reader understand why a character may act a certain way in the story. For example, a character who is shy may not want to talk with a lot of people in a new classroom, but a character who is outgoing may want to talk with many people.

An author typically provides many details about a character so that the reader can learn more about the character's traits, motivations, relationships, and any conflicts they may have in the story. The traits of a character may include how they act and how they look. Characters are often motivated by things that have already happened in their life or how they feel about a topic. The author will often give the reader enough information about the character so that the reader can figure out why the character responds to a situation in a certain way. The author will also often give details about the relationships between characters and points they may conflict on. For example, a character may be good friends with another character; however, the two characters may disagree on where to play outside if one character likes being near the water and the other character does not.

#### EXAMPLE

Read the following description of a character and decide, logically, whether the character is likely to go hiking outdoors:

> Jeremy lived in a high-rise in Chicago. He was studious, and not very athletic. Jeremy preferred to stay indoors and read a book, rather than enjoy outdoor weather.

Based on the description of the character's traits, preferences, and personality, he is not likely to go hiking outdoors. The description indicates that the character prefers reading, rather than enjoying outdoor weather. In addition, the character lives in a tall building in the middle of a large city, in order for him to enjoy the outdoors, he would have to travel away from where he lives. The character is not likely to change his preferences. A situation may lead the character to go hiking, but he is not likely to initiate the action on his own. A description of a character that is likely to go hiking outdoors may include a preference for outdoor activity and living near trails.

### *CHARACTER RELATIONSHIPS*

A relationship is the way one character acts with another character in a story. The characters are often called **major characters** if they have a main part in the story and **minor characters** if they have a smaller part. There are many different kinds of relationships. For example, two children in a story may be friends, but they could be angry with each other, competing with each other, or



Copyright © Mometrix Media. You have been licensed one copy of this document for personal use only. Any other reproduction or redistribution is strictly prohibited. All rights reserved.
This content is provided for test preparation purposes only and does not imply an endorsement by Mometrix of any particular political, scientific, or religious point of view.

helping each other. An author may tell the reader what kind of relationship the characters have. An author might give hints about a relationship. For example, the author may show one child making fun of the other child, which would suggest that the two children do not have a friendly relationship. The author might show one child teaching the other child how to read, which would suggest that the two children have a friendly relationship.

#### EXAMPLE

Read the following sentences and describe the relationship Jill and Anna have:

> Jill came over to Anna and asked if she wanted an apple. "Sure, I'd love one. Thanks," Anna answered. Anna took a bite of the apple and started to chew it. Her chewing was so loud that they both started to laugh.

The author does not tell what the relationship between Jill and Anna is. The reader must figure it out from their actions. These actions are the clues the author gives. Jill asks Anna if she wants an apple. Anna says yes and starts to eat it. Her chewing is very loud. Both Jill and Anna start to laugh. They seem to like each other. Jill seems generous to Anna because she gives Anna an apple. They laugh together, and friends often laugh together. The reader can use personal experience to decide that it seems as though Jill and Anna are friends.

### CHARACTER CHANGES

Characters can change in a multitude of ways throughout a story; however, there are main aspects of a character that change. A character's identifying **characteristics**, such as personality or behavior traits, may change as the result of a prominent event in the story, current **motivations**, and **conflicts**. As conflicts change or are resolved, a character may no longer be motivated by striving toward a goal that was previously important to them. As the plot of a story moves along, characters can constantly change in relation to events that occur. **Relationships** between characters and the points of view of characters may change throughout a story as well.

Each story will have many different types of characters and each of these characters will have a different relationship with other characters. Stories usually have a protagonist, antagonist, and a variety of other characters including round, flat, and stock characters.

#### PROTAGONIST

The main character in a drama, movie, novel, or other fictional text. The author portrays the protagonist in a way that the audience is most like to identify with themselves. The protagonist is generally undertaking some type of personal challenge throughout the story. The author writes the story so that the reader becomes aware of the protagonist's emotions and is generally able to empathize with the personal challenge.

#### ANTAGONIST

The character that actively opposes the protagonist by trying to prevent them from succeeding. The antagonist is usually presented in such a way as to make the audience dislike them, and want them to fail at stopping the protagonist. The protagonist and antagonist oppose each other, so their relationship is almost always one of dislike.

#### FLAT CHARACTERS

Does not have any substantial changes throughout the story. They stay the same despite the conflict, and do not learn any lessons. They are usually minor characters that might interact with the main character in some way.



Copyright © Mometrix Media. You have been licensed one copy of this document for personal use only. Any other reproduction or redistribution is strictly prohibited. All rights reserved.
This content is provided for test preparation purposes only and does not imply an endorsement by Mometrix of any particular political, scientific, or religious point of view.

#### Round Characters

Major characters in the story that will be more fully developed than other minor characters. They will usually encounter some type of conflict that they must overcome, and usually learn a lesson about life or themselves along the way.

#### Stock Characters

Often get their characteristics and mannerisms from stereotypes of people that are widely recognized. These types of characters are often repeated and well-known. Readers should be aware that stereotypes are rarely accurate in reality, and are generally intended to be humorous or dramatic. Some examples are evil stepmothers, unintelligent blondes, rude athletes, and loyal servants.

## Main Idea and Theme

### Key Ideas and Supporting Details

Identifying **key ideas** helps the reader see what a text or story is mostly about. They are the **most important ideas** in a text, and everything else in the text builds around and supports them. Every piece of writing has key ideas. The **supporting details** in a story, such as the characters, events, and settings, will work together to reveal the key ideas. The details are not key ideas, themselves. They make the key ideas clear and show the reader the author's purpose for writing the text.

### Theme

The **theme** of a story, essay, or poem is the lesson that it teaches, or the message the author wants to get across. The theme is linked to the characters, the setting, and the events in a story. A passage can have two or more themes that convey its overall idea.

The theme of a story is not the same as the topic of a story. The topic is what the story is about, but the theme is what a reader is meant to learn. When readers are discussing theme, they can determine both theme topics as well as theme statements.

**Theme topics** are broad ideas that apply to the text. Examples are:

- Love
- The importance of friendship
- Good vs. evil
- The circle of life

Themes may also be complete statements written in sentence form. Examples are:

- Acts of courage can bring positive changes to the world.
- True friendship can withstand the hardest challenges.

Some themes are fairly common. These themes are called **universal themes** and they suggest things about life, society, and human nature.

Themes are very rarely stated in the text. Instead, the reader has to **infer** the theme by reading closely and thinking carefully about what the author is saying.

Themes are an important part of literature because they serve the purpose of teaching the reader or listener a truth about life. The theme is developed by how a character or characters respond to their situations and challenges.



Copyright © Mometrix Media. You have been licensed one copy of this document for personal use only. Any other reproduction or redistribution is strictly prohibited. All rights reserved.
This content is provided for test preparation purposes only and does not imply an endorsement by Mometrix of any particular political, scientific, or religious point of view.

### *EXAMPLE*

Read the following and consider the theme of the excerpt.

> Jeanie arrived at the bake sale early. She bought the biggest cake at the sale. Sally had to work late. When she finally got to the sale, no cakes were left. She got only two cookies. She was lucky to get anything.

The saying "the early bird gets the worm" is one way to explain the theme of the story. In the story we read that Jeanie arrived early at the bake sale and got the biggest cake. But when Sally arrived, all that was left were two cookies. The point of the story is that the early bird gets the worm—the worm in this case is a large cake.

# Types of Texts

## CHILDREN'S LITERATURE

There are types of texts that are specifically meant to be read by children or younger audiences. Children's literature contains many different **genres**, which are categories that texts can be divided into. Some types of children's literature are

- **Folktales** -Songs, stories, myths, or proverbs belonging to a group of people. Often passed down from generation to generation by word of mouth.
- **Fairy tales** are stories that include fictional creatures or characters with fantastical traits and abilities. Fairy tales often end happily and depict the victory of good over evil. The plots and characters in fairy tales are often far-fetched and whimsical.
- **Fables** –Story told (often by a narrator) full of supernatural features like speaking animals. The tale demonstrates a useful truth at the end.
- **Legends** -A story featuring a national or folk hero. Often has a basis in actual fact, but also contains imaginative material.
- **Myth** -A legend or traditional narrative, often based on a historical event. The story reveals something about human behavior or the natural world, and often involves actions of gods.
- **Tall Tales** -A story full of outlandish exaggerations, often humorous and containing heroes who perform impossible acts easily.

## POETRY

### *POET VERSUS SPEAKER*

The author of a poem is called a **poet**. Many poems are written in first person, which means the **stanzas** (groups of lines) include words like "I" and "me." However, the poet is not always the **speaker** of the poem. In a novel, the author can create characters with different points of view. The characters can argue or have different roles to play in telling the story. Similarly, a poet may write a poem from a different point of view or even include more than one voice. The speaker is the voice of the poem, and is not always the same person as the poet him or herself. The reader or listener should know that the person telling the story is a character, and not always a real person.

For example, this excerpt from a poem by Dr. Seuss reads:

> When you think things are bad,
> when you feel sour and blue,
> when you start to get mad...
> you should do what I do!
> Just tell yourself, Duckie,



Copyright © Mometrix Media. You have been licensed one copy of this document for personal use only. Any other reproduction or redistribution is strictly prohibited. All rights reserved.
This content is provided for test preparation purposes only and does not imply an endorsement by Mometrix of any particular political, scientific, or religious point of view.

you're really quite lucky!
Some people are much more...
oh, ever so much more...
oh, muchly much-much more
unlucky than you!

Even though one line has the word "I" in it, the poem is not from the perspective of Dr. Seuss. He is the author of the poem, but not the speaker. The person saying "I" is a character, just like in a story.

### Sensory Language in Poetry

Sensory language is when the author uses descriptive words and specific details that appeal to a reader's senses (sight, touch, taste, hearing, smell, emotion). For example, the author can use scents that the reader is familiar with to help them imagine what the setting of the poem smells and feels like. This use of sensory language is also called **imagery**.

### Rhyme in Poetry

Poets use rhymes to help readers understand poems. Words **rhyme** when they sound similar to each other, especially when the similar sound is at the end of the words, like *cat* and *hat*, or *roar* and *soar*. Rhyming words usually have endings that are spelled the same way, but sometimes they are spelled differently, like *wait* and *hate* or *bear* and *snare*.

Famous poet Shel Silverstein uses rhyme in many of his poems. For example, in his poem "Listen to the Mustn'ts", the last word of the first- and second-lines rhyme with each other, and the last word of the third- and fourth-line rhyme with each other.

Listen to Mustn'ts, child, listen to the Don'ts.
Listen to the Shouldn'ts, the Impossibles, the Won'ts.
Listen to the Never Haves, then listen close to me.
Anything can happen, child, Anything can be.

The pattern of the rhymes in this poem forms a **rhyme scheme**. Sometimes poets use a rhyme scheme that makes every other line of the poem rhyme instead.

### Sound Devices

Sound devices allow authors to add another level to their texts by tapping into the spoken part of language. Authors may use many sound devices to create meaning and help readers understand them better, including:

#### Onomatopoeia

- Appeals to the reader's sense of hearing by using words that copy the noises objects or people make, like sound effects.
- For example, an author might write "The soccer ball whooshed across the field into the goalie's net, scoring the winning point!" The word "whooshed" is an **onomatopoeia** because it mimics the sound of air moving quickly. Because the writer chose to include an onomatopoeia, the reader is able to better picture the action in the sentence.

#### Alliteration, Assonance, and Consonance

- Alliteration, assonance, and consonance all deal with using the same sound throughout a line or sentence. **Alliteration** is the use of words that begin with the **same sound** in a sentence or in a line of poetry. **Assonance** refers to alliteration with a repeated **vowel** sound, whereas **consonance** refers to alliteration with **consonant** sounds.



Copyright © Mometrix Media. You have been licensed one copy of this document for personal use only. Any other reproduction or redistribution is strictly prohibited. All rights reserved.
This content is provided for test preparation purposes only and does not imply an endorsement by Mometrix of any particular political, scientific, or religious point of view.

- For example, the following line contains two sets of alliteration: "I saw a fly fly past my eye, straight into a fresh cherry pie. I felt a flea flee away from my knee and onto the sleeping dog." The first line uses the same sound in the words *I, fly, eye,* and *pie,* which is assonance. The second line uses both assonance and consonance, using the same vowel sound in *flea, flee, knee*, and, *sleeping*. The repeated consonants show up in the words *felt, flea*, and *flee.*

| **Review Video: Alliteration in Everyday Expressions** |
|---|
| Visit mometrix.com/academy and enter code: 462837 |

## DRAMA

Dramas are texts that are written to be performed by people reading the lines or acting the stories out. They can also be presented as monologues (one character speaks), dialogues (two character speak to each other), or pantomimes (body movements are used instead of spoken words). Dramatic texts are called plays or **scripts**, and they are written differently than other texts.

### *TEXT STRUCTURE IN DRAMA*

Plays are divided into **acts** (large units) and **scenes** (small sections inside acts) instead of chapters. There are also **stage directions**, which are instructions from the playwright about where items go, where actors should move, and what the characters should be doing during the scene. Stage directions are usually in italics to set them apart from other parts of the play. When it is time for a character in a play to speak, there will be **character tag** on the left side of the page which shows the name of the character (all letters of the name are capitalized) followed by a colon.

Here is an example of how a page from a play might look:

Title of Play

Act Number

Scene Number

*The setting of the scene is being described here. The reader is being introduced to the characters and the things happening around them. Characters will enter speak to one another during the scene.*

CHARACTER 1:

I am speaking. These are words I say. *(stage directions)* I am still speaking.

CHARACTER 2 *enters and does something.*

CHARACTER 2:

Now I am speaking. This is my dialogue.

### *DIALOGUE AND STAGE DIRECTIONS*

**Dialogue** refers to what the characters say in a play when they are talking to each other, talking to themselves, or even talking to the audience. The type of speech, word choice, and accent a character uses is specific to the role he is playing. For example, a person cast to play a cowboy would have certain words in his vocabulary that a character from a big city in the North would not have.

A playwright also uses stage directions to make the play flow smoothly. Character interaction helps the viewer to understand the mood of the scene. If two characters are confrontational, the viewer is



Copyright © Mometrix Media. You have been licensed one copy of this document for personal use only. Any other reproduction or redistribution is strictly prohibited. All rights reserved.
This content is provided for test preparation purposes only and does not imply an endorsement by Mometrix of any particular political, scientific, or religious point of view.

aware that there is some type of conflict occurring. Stage directions create order when all the characters are on stage together.

## Informational Text

### *Controlling Idea*

The controlling idea, also called the main idea or thesis, of a passage is usually located in the first paragraph or two of text. Having the controlling idea near the beginning of the passage allows the author to grab the reader's attention and let them know what the rest of the passage will discuss.

To find the controlling idea in a passage, there are questions the reader can ask while reading: What is this passage about? What does the author want the reader to know about the topic? The supporting details will provide evidence that the controlling idea is correct and are found in the body of a passage. The supporting details often provide examples of the controlling idea.

### *Supporting Details*

Provide evidence and backing for the main point. All texts contain details, but they are only classified as supporting details when they serve to reinforce some larger point. Supporting details are most commonly found in informative and persuasive texts. In some cases, they will be clearly indicated with words like **for example** or **for instance**, or they will begin with words like **first**, **second**, and **last**. However, these special words are not a requirement. As a reader, it is important to consider whether the author's supporting details really back up his or her main point. Supporting details can be factual and correct but still not relevant to the author's point. Sometimes, supporting details can seem important but they might not support the main idea in the story well because they are based on opinion that cannot be proven.

#### Example

Decide whether the following sentence is the main point or a supporting point of a text, and state where the information would be placed in an outline:

> One type of horseback riding, bareback horseback riding, involves sitting on a moving horse without a saddle and grasping the horse's mane.

This sentence is a supporting point, with the main point of the entire text likely about horseback riding in general. As a supporting point, this sentence would go further down in an outline, next to any numeral after numeral I. This sentence can be followed by additional sub-points that further explain the concept of bareback horseback riding. When a supporting point is used to clarify a main point or topic, the supporting point helps to break the topic down into smaller pieces.

### *Structural Features of Informational Text*

Texts which intend to inform the reader about a topic are often accompanied by visual aids or graphics. Some common examples are listed below.

- **Insets and sidebars** show additional information related to the text in boxes or on the sides of the page. Insets can contain pictures or text, and sometimes have different colored backgrounds or font types to make them stand out from the text.
- **Visual aids** include features like diagrams, graphs, and charts. These can help the user think about information in a different way. They do this by visually presenting the relationship between the information in the text.
- **Timelines** are a visual aid which show how events from the text happened over time, and usually contain dates, locations, or other related information.



Copyright © Mometrix Media. You have been licensed one copy of this document for personal use only. Any other reproduction or redistribution is strictly prohibited. All rights reserved.
This content is provided for test preparation purposes only and does not imply an endorsement by Mometrix of any particular political, scientific, or religious point of view.

- **Tables** are visual aids that organize information in a way that shows the relationship between the information. Tables are made using rows and columns, and the pieces in the rows and columns are called cells. Usually, the first row or column will contain a title or heading that categorizes or defines the other cells in that row or column.
- **Bullet points** list items separately, making facts and ideas easier to see and understand.
- **Numbers** can also be used to list separate items. Usually, numbers are used to show that the items are part of a sequence. For example, in a list of instructions, each instruction may be numbered to show the reader the order in which each instruction should be completed.
- **Italics** are a formatting technique that makes text appear slanted. Italics can be used to emphasize text because they cause the text to look different and lead the reader to notice it more easily. Italics are also often used in fiction to show that text is part of a character's thoughts. They are also commonly used to show that a word or section of text is written in a foreign language.
- **Boldface** is a way to format text to make it stand out. Boldface, or bold, text can be used to emphasize a word, phrase, or idea. Boldface can also be used to let the reader know that they can find more information about a term in a glossary, sidebar, or other feature of the text.

## ARGUMENTATIVE TEXTS

### *IDENTIFYING THE CLAIM*

In a persuasive or argumentative text, the author is writing in order to make and support a claim. A claim is similar to the key idea of an informational text. However, a claim can be argued, which means that some readers may not agree with it. The author of the text will need to use the body of the text to support the claim and show readers why they should agree with it. To identify the claim of a text, first identify the topic. Then, read the introduction text to see what the author writes about the topic.

The claim should be clearly stated in the introduction. However, if the claim is still not clear, read the body to see what kind of evidence the author uses to support the claim. The way that the author gives and applies evidence may also show what the claim of the text is.

#### CALL TO ACTION

Another strategy is to look for a call to action in the text. A call to action is a statement that instructs the reader to do something after reading the text. Often, the call to action will tell the reader to do something that shows that he or she agrees with the author's claim. For example, if an author's claim is that reading is better than watching a movie, the author may include a call to action that says "Turn off the TV and dig in to a new book today!" By including this statement, the author is telling the readers to show their agreement by choosing to read rather than watch a movie.

### *IDENTIFYING HOW THE AUTHOR SUPPORTS A CLAIM*

In a persuasive or argumentative text, the author must use information to support his or her claim. This information is called evidence. Below are common types of evidence an author may use to support a claim:

- **Facts:** Authors may use facts that show that their claim is true. For example, a claim that fish are better pets than dogs can be supported by the fact that fish cannot make a mess inside a house.



Copyright © Mometrix Media. You have been licensed one copy of this document for personal use only. Any other reproduction or redistribution is strictly prohibited. All rights reserved.
This content is provided for test preparation purposes only and does not imply an endorsement by Mometrix of any particular political, scientific, or religious point of view.

- **Examples:** Authors may give examples of events or experiences that suggest that their claim is true. For example, an author may claim that people should exercise because it will make them healthier. The author could give an example of how exercise can improve a person's health in order to support this claim.
- **Quotes:** An author can support a claim by using quotes from other people or texts. If the person or text makes a statement that shows that the author's claim is true, the author can include that quote in his or her text. When authors include quotes in their work, they must always tell the reader where the quote came from.

The author must use enough evidence to support the claim. If the evidence does not fully support the claim in the text, then the author must continue working to find evidence for the claim. The evidence used to support a claim must also be believable and come from a reliable source.

### *Identifying the Intended Audience*

Authors of persuasive and argumentative texts want to convince others to agree with a claim or take a certain action. Because of this, they will often write to a specific audience. Often, the target audience will include people who disagree with the author's claim. The author's desire is to give these people information that will lead them to change their minds or actions.

#### Strategies for Identifying the Intended Audience

One way to identify the intended audience of a persuasive or argumentative text is to first identify the author's claim. Then, consider who would disagree with the author's claim. This group of people is likely the group that the author wants to persuade.

Another way to identify the audience is to look for clues in the text. Sometimes, authors will clearly state which people are included in the intended audience. For example, imagine that an author includes the statement, "Teachers should reward their students every time they make a good grade on a test." This shows that the text is written to persuade teachers who do not already reward their students for good test grades. Similarly, a call to action may show who the target audience is by instructing the members of the audience to take a certain action.

# Point of View

## Point of View

Authors choose which character tells the story they are writing. This is called **point of view**. The point of view affects the story in many ways. There are three general types of point of view:

### *First Person*

- Tells a story through the eyes of one character.
- Uses the pronouns 'I,' 'me,' 'we,' and 'my.'
- The reader gets only one side of the story, without any other angles on what may have happened in the text

### *Second Person*

- Tells a story using the pronoun 'you.'
- The least common point of view.

### *Third Person*

- Tells a story about a character or group of characters from an outside viewpoint.
- Uses the words 'her', 'his,' 'they,' or a name to talk about a character or characters.



Copyright © Mometrix Media. You have been licensed one copy of this document for personal use only. Any other reproduction or redistribution is strictly prohibited. All rights reserved.
This content is provided for test preparation purposes only and does not imply an endorsement by Mometrix of any particular political, scientific, or religious point of view.

- A common way to show action in a story which allows the author to easily and realistically tell a story from more than one person's viewpoint.
- Gives readers a more complete view of a story as it is told from many different perspectives.
  - Gives readers a more complete view of a story as it is told from many different perspectives.

# Drawing Conclusions and Making Inferences

## Making Inferences and Conclusions

An **inference** is a **conclusion** or generalization that the reader makes based on the information provided within a text. Certain facts are included to help a reader come to a specific conclusion.

For example, a story may open with a man trudging through the snow on a cold winter day, dragging a sled behind him. The reader can infer from the setting of the story that the man is wearing heavy winter clothes in order to stay warm. Information is implied based on the setting of a story, which is why setting is an important element of the text. If the same man in the example was trudging down a beach on a hot summer day, dragging a surf board behind him, the reader would assume that the man is not wearing heavy clothes. The reader makes inferences based on their own experiences and the information presented to them in the story.

Readers may come to their own conclusion about a topic, or the author may state a conclusion at the end of a story. When readers are in the middle of a story, they can predict what will happen at the end of it based on the events that have occurred so far and the typical characteristics that have been presented by the author up to that point. A reader needs to consider all of the information that an author has presented, including the main point and supporting points, to make logical conclusions and inferences about the story.

Sometimes interpreting the information in a sentence can be difficult, especially if the reader is unfamiliar with some of the words used in a sentence. Drawing a picture of what is actually happening in the sentence can help, along with looking at the words that the reader does understand in the sentence. By taking a pen or pencil and underlining important information in a sentence, the reader can better understand what the author is trying to say and draw a clearer conclusion from that. Using context clues, or wording in a sentence, is an important way to identify what the author is talking about in the story. An author will often leave blanks for the reader to fill in on their own, using information that has been presented up to that point in the story.

### *Example*

Describe what can be inferred from the following sentences:

> Sometimes after a big storm, the beaches are covered with dead fish, seaweed, broken shells, and pieces of wood. Most seaweed is brown or gold, but there are often pieces of white seaweed. If people visit the beaches, the white seaweed disappears very quickly. It makes a delicious pudding.

To make an inference a reader needs to look for clues in a text. The author does not tell an inference directly; the author hints at one. Here the text says that fish, seaweed, and shells are on the beach after a storm. It also says that some of the seaweed is white and adds that the white seaweed is used for pudding. Another clue is that the white seaweed disappears quickly if people visit the beaches. The inference that a reader can figure out is that the people take the seaweed. It disappears quickly because it can be used to make a delicious pudding.



Copyright © Mometrix Media. You have been licensed one copy of this document for personal use only. Any other reproduction or redistribution is strictly prohibited. All rights reserved.
This content is provided for test preparation purposes only and does not imply an endorsement by Mometrix of any particular political, scientific, or religious point of view.

### EXAMPLE

Read the following two sentences and draw a conclusion based on the text:

> Sarah worked hard on her science project. Her presentation of the science project to the class went well.

Based on the two sentences, the reader can conclude that Sarah will receive a high grade on her science project. The reader knows that Sarah put a great deal of time and effort into her project and that the actual presentation of the project was successful. Based on these facts, the reader can assume that the teacher will appreciate and reward Sarah's effort. This conclusion can be drawn based on the reader's knowledge of how high grades are obtained and their own previous experience with school projects. The reader can assume that Sarah's assessment of her presentation is accurate, that the presentation did indeed conform to high expectations. When a conclusion is drawn based on information the reader is given in a text, the conclusion is called an *inference*.

### EXAMPLE

Read the following sentence. Draw a conclusion based upon the information presented.

> "A rosy-faced servant-maid opened the door, and smiled as she took the letter which he silently offered."

The reader can conclude, based on the sentence, that the servant-maid is friendly. The words "rosy-faced" and "smiled" lead the reader to this conclusion. People who are friendly are often described as having rosy complexions and smiling as a common sign of pleasantness. The reader can also assume, from the sentence, that the letter does not present any threat or unpleasantness to the servant-maid. The person presenting the letter does not have anything to say upon offering it, so perhaps he is waiting to see how the servant-maid will react.

When interpreting a sentence, always look for key words that describe a character. The author carefully crafts a description of each character, to form a picture in the reader's mind about what the character is like.

### FACTS AND OPINIONS

Writers and readers must always be aware of the difference between fact and opinion. A **fact** can be tested and proven to be true. An **opinion**, on the other hand, is someone's personal thoughts or feelings. Opinions are often not changed by information. If an author writes that a newborn elephant is about five times taller than a newborn giraffe, then he or she is stating a fact. If the author writes that giraffes are more interesting than elephants, then he or she is giving an opinion because this cannot be proven to be true or false. Opinions are often supported by facts. For instance, the author might use a comparison between the way that giraffes eat and the way elephants eat as evidence of how giraffes are more interesting. An opinion supported by facts tends to be more convincing. On the other hand, when authors support their opinions with other opinions, readers should seriously think about and read the argument carefully to see whether it is logical and trustworthy.

**Review Video: Distinguishing Fact and Opinion**
Visit mometrix.com/academy and enter code: 870899



Copyright © Mometrix Media. You have been licensed one copy of this document for personal use only. Any other reproduction or redistribution is strictly prohibited. All rights reserved.
This content is provided for test preparation purposes only and does not imply an endorsement by Mometrix of any particular political, scientific, or religious point of view.

# Graphic Features in Texts

## PRINT AND GRAPHIC FEATURES

An author may show information in a chart, a graph, in paragraph format, or as a list. Information may also be shown in a picture or a diagram. The way an author chooses to show information is often based on the purpose of the text and the audience that the text is meant to reach.

A reader may be asked to answer questions based on the graphic by itself, how the graphic relates to the text, or how the text would best be shown in a graphic form. Some common examples of graphics are cause and effect organizers, circle graphs, bar graphs, illustrations, and diagrams.

### *CAUSE AND EFFECT GRAPHIC ORGANIZERS*

Cause-and-effect graphic organizers are often used to map the **elements of a story**. A reader might read a story about a string of events and then be asked to correctly fill in either the **cause** or **effect** of an event in the story.

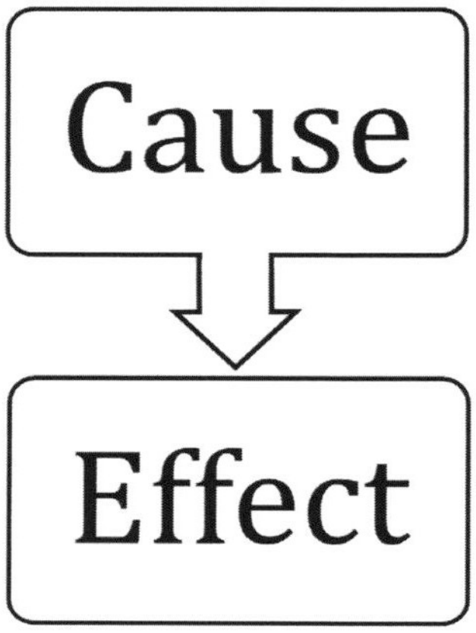


#### EXAMPLE

Read the following excerpt from *Ramona Quimby, Age 8* by Beverly Cleary and decide what the cause of the hectic morning at the Quimby house is.

> With all four members of the family leaving at different times in different directions, mornings were flurried in the Quimby household.



Copyright © Mometrix Media. You have been licensed one copy of this document for personal use only. Any other reproduction or redistribution is strictly prohibited. All rights reserved.
This content is provided for test preparation purposes only and does not imply an endorsement by Mometrix of any particular political, scientific, or religious point of view.

A **cause and effect** graphic organizer for this excerpt might look something like this:

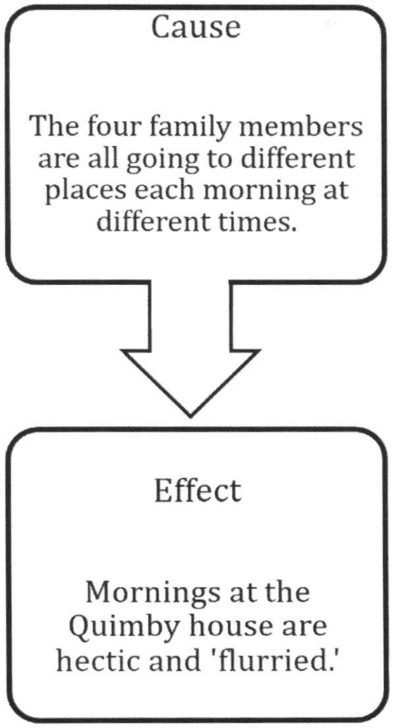


### *Circle Graphs*

Circle graphs, also called pie charts, are often used to represent information that can be shown as **parts of a whole**. For example, this graph shows the results of people being asked about their favorite color:

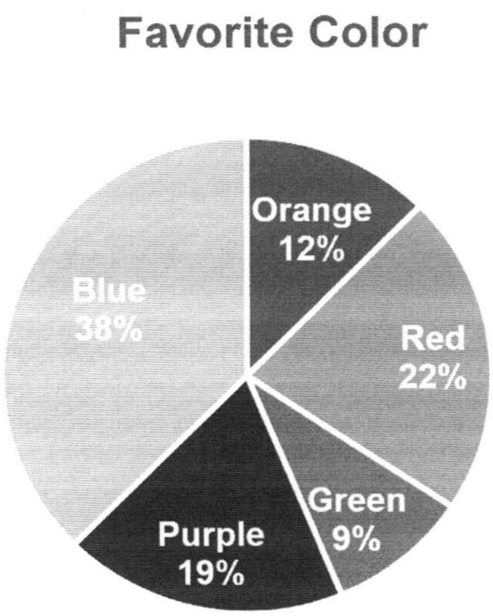




Copyright © Mometrix Media. You have been licensed one copy of this document for personal use only. Any other reproduction or redistribution is strictly prohibited. All rights reserved.
This content is provided for test preparation purposes only and does not imply an endorsement by Mometrix of any particular political, scientific, or religious point of view.

### *Bar Graphs*

Bar graphs are used to show information about **numbers**. For example, this graph is a different way of representing the same results as those in the circle graph.

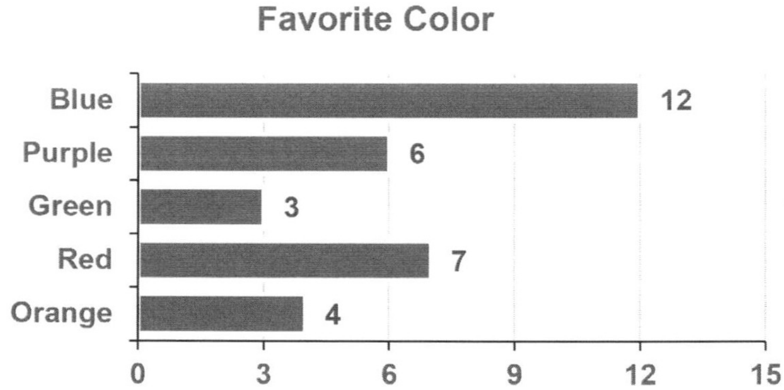


### *Illustrations and Photographs*

Authors may choose to include **illustrations** or **photographs** (or both) with their texts. These two image types both show something from the text or give more information about the text.

Illustrations are drawings of an object. They may be based on reality, or they may represent an artist's abstract idea. For example, this is an illustration of a 1903 automobile:

Photographs are pictures of objects. They are generally extremely realistic, and most often show an object as it actually existed at that moment in time. For example, this is a photograph of a 1917 automobile:

Both illustrations and photographs give the reader another way to relate to and understand the text. The reader may be asked how the image relates to the text, what type of caption the image should be given, or why the author chose to include the image with the text.

### *Diagrams*

Diagrams are used to show information in a visual way. There are many different types of diagrams, including:



Copyright © Mometrix Media. You have been licensed one copy of this document for personal use only. Any other reproduction or redistribution is strictly prohibited. All rights reserved.
This content is provided for test preparation purposes only and does not imply an endorsement by Mometrix of any particular political, scientific, or religious point of view.

Diagrams that show the parts of an object, how they work together, or how they should be put together. This is an example of a diagram which shows how gears turn together

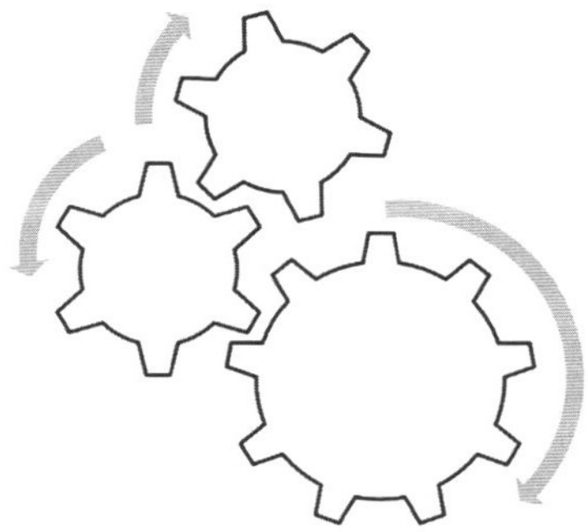

Diagrams that show how information is related are called **Venn Diagrams**. These are ways to visually see the way in which two different ideas overlap. This is an example of a Venn Diagram comparing cats and dogs:

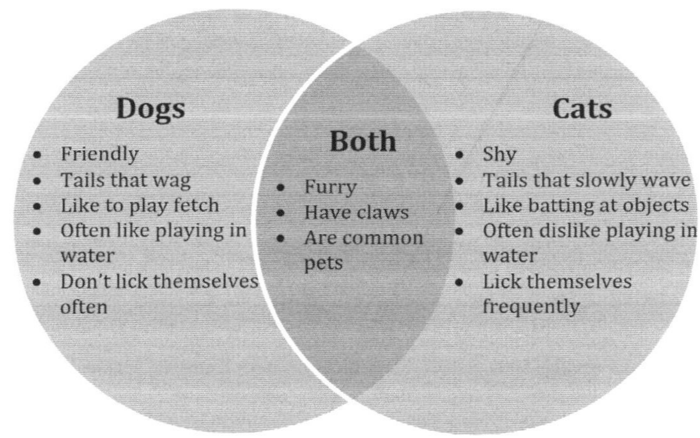


# Organizational Patterns in Texts

## Organizational Patterns

Authors want to have an effective text that the reader can understand. If ideas do not follow a **logical order**, the reader will become confused and not know what the author is trying to say. When writing, there are a variety of ways that an author can choose to organize a written work. It is important to choose the pattern that **best presents** the information, as not all patterns will work for every piece of writing. An author may organize ideas according to a timeline, cause and effect, or description of an event or setting.

### Order of Importance

The author puts the information in the text in order of what is most important. Order of importance can be either increasing or decreasing, depending on how the writer wants to structure the work.

### Chronological Order

The author organizes the progression of events based upon when they occurred and what was included in each step of the story. By organizing the text in this way the author presents all



Copyright © Mometrix Media. You have been licensed one copy of this document for personal use only. Any other reproduction or redistribution is strictly prohibited. All rights reserved.
This content is provided for test preparation purposes only and does not imply an endorsement by Mometrix of any particular political, scientific, or religious point of view.

necessary information about the six questions readers can ask to help themselves understand the text: who, what, when, where, why, and how.

### Problem and Solution

The author presents some information as a problem and then discusses a solution or attempted solution to that problem. In problem and solution, there is generally one main problem, but that one problem may have several possible solutions.

For example, suppose Billy wants a new video game but does not have the money. There are several possible solutions to this. He might try asking his mom to buy it for him. If that does not work, he could offer to do small jobs to earn enough money to buy it. A third possibility might be to wait until his birthday and ask for it then.

### Cause and Effect

The author will write about relationship between two events that occur, where the second event occurs as a result of the first.

For example, a text may discuss a school policy stating that when a student is late to school too many times, they receive a detention. Later in the text, we might see a student repeatedly arriving late to school, after which he is given a detention. In this example, the **cause** is the student being late to school, and the **effect** is the student receiving a detention.

### Compare and Contrast

The author will show similarities and differences between items or events.

For example, the author may write about cats and dogs. They might start by giving a brief description of the two. Then they will want to point out all of the similarities, such as; they both have tails, and both are kept as pets. Next, they will explain the differences, such as; dogs are canines, while cats are felines. They will try to provide as much detail as possible about both the similarities and the differences.

Ideas may vary in complexity, in addition to their main point. Topics of debate, or issues, may have pros and cons. By comparing the positive and negative aspects of each view, the reader can better understand how the viewpoints are similar and different.

#### *Example*

Read the following two viewpoints and compare and contrast how the two viewpoints are similar and different:

> (1) Basketball is the best sport to play, because a participant can be part of a team and excel individually.
>
> (2) In basketball, players must work together to execute plays and achieve points for the team.

In the first viewpoint, the author states that basketball is the best sport to play, whereas in the second viewpoint, the author simply states how the game is played. The first viewpoint also refers to an individual player's performance, while the second viewpoint focuses on the fact that the team needs to score points together in order to win the game. The first viewpoint is trying to convince the reader, while the second viewpoint is explaining how the game is played. Yes, an individual may excel at scoring points, as indicated in the first viewpoint, but the second viewpoint emphasizes the



Copyright © Mometrix Media. You have been licensed one copy of this document for personal use only. Any other reproduction or redistribution is strictly prohibited. All rights reserved.
This content is provided for test preparation purposes only and does not imply an endorsement by Mometrix of any particular political, scientific, or religious point of view.

fact that plays need to be done together in order to score points for the entire team. Two differing viewpoints will often overlap in relation to the topic that they are discussing.

### *Identifying Organizational Patterns*

#### Example

Read the following paragraph from a news story and describe how the author organizes information in the story:

> The parade in honor of the town's 200th anniversary began at the corner of 57th Street at 9:00 a.m. on Saturday morning. Members of the fire department led the parade, dressed in their bright red hats and heavy yellow coats. At 9:15 a.m., members of the high school band gave a performance.

The news story uses chronological order organize ideas. The reader is given information about what type of event occurred, when the event occurred, what the event was about, and who was included.

#### Example

Identify organizational pattern that is used in the following sentence from *Morte d'Arthur* by Sir Thomas Malory:

> The king had given his promise, so he was obliged to agree.

The text structure of cause and effect is used in this sentence. The cause in the sentence is that the king gave his promise, and the effect is that he had to agree.

### *Patterns of Organization for Stories*

Different forms of writing benefit from particular patterns of organization. For instance, simple stories usually follow a chronological organization, but they can use other structures. Some literary works start in the middle of the action, then go back to the beginning of the story, and then through the events to the end. The organization plays a big role in keeping information interesting or surprising. The author can use these patterns to emphasize or even hide information from the reader until the right time. In informational texts, the author usually chooses a structure to help emphasize his or her purpose. This includes cause and effect, compare and contrast, or a thesis method that argues for specific reasons.



Copyright © Mometrix Media. You have been licensed one copy of this document for personal use only. Any other reproduction or redistribution is strictly prohibited. All rights reserved.
This content is provided for test preparation purposes only and does not imply an endorsement by Mometrix of any particular political, scientific, or religious point of view.

# Practice Test #1

*Refer to the following for questions 1–10:*

**A Garden in the Desert**

(1) Barry lives one street up and four houses down from his best friend, Manolo. Barry, his parents, and his older brother Ricardo have lived in the small ranch house for as long as he can remember. Manolo's family moved into their house a few months before Manolo was born. At that time, 10 years ago, their housing development was only five square blocks. About 250 small, one-story houses dotted the streets. Today, their housing development is three times as big and is considered an actual neighborhood. It is called Cypress Heights.

(2) There are no cypresses or any other kinds of trees in Cypress Heights. The neighborhood was built near a desert. It has no heights and no hills – just flat stretches of paved road and concrete sidewalks. Grass sprouts up between the cracks in the sidewalks but refuses to take root on lawns. Flowers also have a hard time growing in Barry and Manolo's hot and dusty neighborhood. The only plants that grow around most of the houses are patches of ragged-looking weeds.

(3) In contrast to the dusty lawns, most of the ranch houses are very well kept. The outsides of the houses are freshly painted, and many lawns are decorated with bird baths and patio furniture. The lack of gardens and lawns, however, makes the neighborhood look dusty, downtrodden, and old. Without grass roots to knit a protective net in the soil, the wind picks up dirt and blows it all over the roads, roofs, and sidewalks. After a windy day, everything in Cypress Heights is covered in brown and gray dust.

(4) Manolo and Barry love living in Cypress Heights because their houses are so close, and each boy can easily get to the other's house. A short fence surrounds Manolo's backyard. Manolo can jump over the fence and walk along the path in the neighbor's backyard to Barry's street. From there, Manolo can walk past three houses to get to Barry's. The fence around Barry's backyard is too high to jump over and too smooth to climb, so Barry has to stick to the streets to get to Manolo's house.

(5) One summer day, Barry rode his bike over to Manolo's house. He brought a backpack with a picnic lunch. "Let's go to the playground at the school," said Barry. "I have two peanut butter and jelly sandwiches and two juice boxes for lunch. We can stay there all afternoon."

(6) "Sounds good," said Manolo. His older sister was watching him while his mother was at work. He asked his sister, Rosa, for permission.

(7) "Just be back before five o'clock," said Rosa. "Mom should be home by then."

(8) Barry and Manolo's school was about a mile away. It was a long, brown, one-story building with big windows and a large play set in the front. In the back were two sets of train tracks. Usually, the trains only ran at night, but every so often a



Copyright © Mometrix Media. You have been licensed one copy of this document for personal use only. Any other reproduction or redistribution is strictly prohibited. All rights reserved.
This content is provided for test preparation purposes only and does not imply an endorsement by Mometrix of any particular political, scientific, or religious point of view.

freight train would pass the school during the day, making the windows rattle and the children rush from their seats to watch it.

(9) On their way to the schoolyard, they passed a house that had just been sold a few weeks earlier. In the yard, instead of dusty weeds, was white gravel. Dotted around the lawn were different cactus plants. Barry and Manolo stopped their bikes and stared at the lawn in surprise. "Wow, this yard looks great," said Barry. "But I don't want cactus plants in my yard. What if you ran into one while playing tag? That would hurt!"

(10) "There are other plants that work in this area," said a voice from behind a large cactus.

(11) A woman with short brown hair stepped out from behind the cactus and walked over to Barry and Manolo. She had a wide-brimmed hat on her head. "We planted cacti because they don't need much water," said the woman with a smile. She waved her hand toward her house. "It is too expensive to water plants or a lawn. But there are other drought-resistant plants that will do well here."

(12) "What kind of plant is 'drought resistant'?" asked Manolo.

(13) "Basically, it is a plant that doesn't need much water," said the woman. "Plants like lavender, aloe, lamb's ear, and oriental yew are also drought-resistant. I have some of those in pots ready to be planted. If you promise to take care of them, I can give you some to plant in your yards."

(14) "Sure!" said Barry and Manolo at once.

(15) The woman motioned to the boys to follow her behind her house. She put several small plants in a low, flat box attached to the back of her bicycle. She strapped down the plants and climbed on the seat. "Lead the way," she said.

(16) "Thank you," said Barry. "By the way, I'm Barry and this is Manolo."

(17) "I'm Mrs. Juarez," said the woman. "Nice to meet you."

(18) "Wait a minute," said Barry. "You just moved in. Shouldn't we give presents to you?"

(19) "That's okay," laughed Mrs. Juarez. "I don't have any more room in my garden, so you are doing me a favor by taking them. But I will accept a cold drink after the bike ride!"

(20) "Sounds good," said Barry. The three of them headed towards the boys' houses, ready to break ground on their new gardens.

**1. What is the main objective of paragraphs 2 and 3?**

a. To describe Manolo's house
b. To describe Barry's house
c. To describe Manolo's and Barry's friendship
d. To describe Manolo's and Barry's neighborhood



Copyright © Mometrix Media. You have been licensed one copy of this document for personal use only. Any other reproduction or redistribution is strictly prohibited. All rights reserved.
This content is provided for test preparation purposes only and does not imply an endorsement by Mometrix of any particular political, scientific, or religious point of view.

**2. What is strange about the name of Barry's and Manolo's neighborhood: Cypress Heights?**

a. There are no Cypress trees and the land is flat
b. The trees in Cypress Heights are actually oak and maple trees
c. Cypress Heights is located in a valley
d. There is no such thing as a Cypress tree

**3. Which sentence in paragraph 3 showed that Cypress Heights residents care about how their houses look?**

a. "The outsides of the houses are freshly painted, and many lawns are decorated with bird baths and patio furniture"
b. "The lack of gardens and lawns, however, makes the neighborhood look dusty, downtrodden, and old"
c. "Without grass roots to knit a protective net in the soil, the wind picks up dirt and blows it all over the roads, roofs, and sidewalks"
d. "After a windy day, everything in Cypress Heights is covered in brown and gray dust"

**4. Why do Barry and Manolo like living close to each other?**

a. Because it is convenient for them to visit each other
b. Because Barry's fence is too high to climb
c. Because their bikes don't work
d. Because Manolo has a shorter walk

**5. Who did the boys meet on their way to the schoolyard?**

a. Barry's parents
b. Mrs. Juarez
c. Rosa, Manolo's sister
d. Manolo's mother

**6. What are "drought-resistant" plants?**

a. Plants that can live in very hot climates
b. Plants that can live in very cold climates
c. Plants that can live in very dry climates
d. Plants that can live in very wet climates

**7. Instead of grass, what did Mrs. Juarez put on her lawn to keep dust and dirt from blowing around?**

a. Lavender
b. Yucca
c. Aloe
d. Gravel

**8. What did Barry mean when he said, "You just moved in. Shouldn't we give presents to you?"**

a. Mrs. Juarez was too busy to give presents
b. Traditionally, new neighbors receive gifts, not give them
c. Mrs. Juarez doesn't know Barry and Manolo well enough to know what they want
d. Barry and Manolo shouldn't take gifts from strangers



Copyright © Mometrix Media. You have been licensed one copy of this document for personal use only. Any other reproduction or redistribution is strictly prohibited. All rights reserved.
This content is provided for test preparation purposes only and does not imply an endorsement by Mometrix of any particular political, scientific, or religious point of view.

**9. In paragraph 3, what does the word "knit" mean?**

a. Join together tightly
b. Make clothing
c. Grow grass
d. Make nets

**10. What phrase best sums up the lesson Mrs. Juarez taught Manolo and Barry?**

a. Good friends turn up in unlikely places
b. Cookies will help you make friends
c. With the right plants, gardens can grow anywhere
d. With the right tools, gardens can grow anywhere

*Refer to the passage "Little White Lily" for questions 11–13.*

"Little White Lily" by George MacDonald

Little White Lily
Sat by a stone,
Drooping and waiting
Till the sun shone.
Little White Lily
Sunshine has fed;
Little White Lily
Is lifting her head.

Little White Lily
Said: "It is good
Little White Lily's
Clothing and food."
Little White Lily
Dressed like a bride!
Shining with
whiteness,
And crownèd beside!

Little White Lily
Drooping with pain,
Waiting and waiting
For the wet rain.
Little White Lily
Holdeth her cup;
Rain is fast falling
And filling it up.

Little White Lily
Said: "Good again,
When I am thirsty
To have the nice rain.
Now I am stronger,
Now I am cool;
Heat cannot burn me,
My veins are so full."

Little White Lily
Smells very sweet;
On her head sunshine,
Rain at her feet.
Thanks to the
sunshine,
Thanks to the rain,
Little White Lily
Is happy again.



Copyright © Mometrix Media. You have been licensed one copy of this document for personal use only. Any other reproduction or redistribution is strictly prohibited. All rights reserved.
This content is provided for test preparation purposes only and does not imply an endorsement by Mometrix of any particular political, scientific, or religious point of view.

**11. What can the reader infer based on the poem "Little White Lily"?**

a. Lilies always grow by stones.
b. Lilies need to drink water in the evening.
c. Lilies will suffer without sunshine and rain.
d. Lilies are most commonly white.

**12. The poet describes the lily as being "dressed like a bride." Why did the poet use this simile?**

a. It tells the reader that the lily was feeling nervous and excited.
b. It shows the reader that people were celebrating the lily.
c. It allows the reader to understand that the lily has layers of petals.
d. It helps the reader imagine the lily by comparing it to a wedding dress.

**13. In lines 25 through 40, what type of voice does the poet's word choice create?**

a. Depressed
b. Thankful
c. Persuasive
d. Silly

*Refer to the passage "Jack's First Christmas in Africa" to answer questions 14-18.*

**Jack's First Christmas in Africa**

(1) "Hi, Jack," said Mom. "How was your day?"

(2) "Fine, I guess," sighed ten-year-old Jack.

(3) "Is everything all right? You don't sound very convincing."

(4) "Yes, Mom, everything's fine."

(5) Really, though, Jack wasn't fine. He was homesick. He and his parents had moved to Africa six months earlier to be missionaries. Africa was very different than America, but most of the time Jack was happy. He had made friends at the school, he was getting used to the bizarre food, and even living in a hut had become enjoyable. But now it was close to Christmas, and Jack missed America more than ever.

(6) Some of the African people didn't even celebrate Christmas, and the ones who did had very different traditions. There were no authentic Christmas trees, no ornaments, and definitely no snow. He wouldn't be enjoying any of his mom's special Christmas cookies because there was no way to get the ingredients needed to bake them. And just what kind of present did Jack expect to get? No new video games, no new skateboard, no new toys at all. None of these things were available in the little village in the middle of the African jungle.

(7) Then, one day at school, their class began talking about Christmas.

(8) "Tell us, Jack. How do you celebrate Christmas in America?" said Wahid.

(9) "Well, first we put up a Christmas tree in our home."

(10) "A Christmas tree?" asked Jalil. "I have never heard of such a thing."

(11) "It's an evergreen tree, one that never loses its leaves. We hang all sorts of decorations all over it, even lights," said Jack.



Copyright © Mometrix Media. You have been licensed one copy of this document for personal use only. Any other reproduction or redistribution is strictly prohibited. All rights reserved.
This content is provided for test preparation purposes only and does not imply an endorsement by Mometrix of any particular political, scientific, or religious point of view.

(12) Jack's classmates listened in amazement to all that Jack had to share about Christmas in America. He told them about all the great food they ate and wrapping presents for his parents in beautiful red, green, silver, and gold paper. He told them about all the family get-togethers, the caroling on the cold winter nights, and the stockings filled with candy and all kinds of treats. He even told them about the special candlelight service they always attended on Christmas Eve.

(13) "Christmas is really about giving, and spending time with friends and family," said Jack.

(14) Finally, a week later, it was the last day of school before the Christmas holidays would start. Jack moved extra slow when he awoke, wishing more than ever he could just stay in his bed. He didn't want to celebrate Christmas in Africa. It just wasn't the same. He dreaded going to school, but he knew he had no choice.

(15) When Jack walked into his classroom, he couldn't believe his eyes. There before him was a Christmas tree! It wasn't the kind of tree he had in America, but it was a tree, and it was covered in decorations, homemade versions of the ones Jack had described to his class. There were presents under the tree, wrapped in paper that had been painted. The colors were red and green with accents of gold and silver. On the table, there were several dozen special African cookies, along with some punch. The students had even cut up tiny pieces of paper and strewn them all over the floor to look like snow.

(16) "Surprise, Jack!" said Wahid. "We wanted to bring American Christmas to you here in Africa."

(17) "Yes," said Jalil. "We know you miss your home, but we are glad you are here to celebrate Christmas with us this year."

(18) "Open your present, Jack," said Ourja.

(19) Jack tore the paper off the present and found a mitt and ball for playing a native African stick game.

(20) Jack smiled. "Thanks, guys," said Jack. "It looks like it's going to be a merry Christmas after all!"

**14. Read the definitions for *accent* below (adapted from Merriam-Webster).**

| **accent** \ ak-sent \ noun<br><br>1. a way of speaking typical of a particular group of people<br>2. a greater stress placed on a musical tone<br>3. an object used for emphasis as part of a design<br>4. a special concern or attention |
|---|

**Which definition of *accent* is used in Paragraph 15?**

a. Definition 1
b. Definition 2
c. Definition 3
d. Definition 4



Copyright © Mometrix Media. You have been licensed one copy of this document for personal use only. Any other reproduction or redistribution is strictly prohibited. All rights reserved.
This content is provided for test preparation purposes only and does not imply an endorsement by Mometrix of any particular political, scientific, or religious point of view.

**15. Based on the events at the end of "Jack's First Christmas in Africa," what is most likely to happen next?**

a. Jack will ask his mother to bake her special cookies to give to his classmates.
b. Jack will still dread waking up tomorrow because he is not in America for Christmas.
c. Jack will use his Christmas gift to play the native African stick game with his classmates.
d. Jack will not eat the special African cookies because they are not the ones his mom makes.

**16. How does line 13 in "Jack's First Christmas in Africa" show the theme of the story?**

a. Jack recognizes that friendship and time with others are more important than traditions.
b. Jack realizes that he can make new friends by sharing common Christmas traditions.
c. Jack decides to use his experiences to help his family adjust to living in a new country.
d. Jack plans to surprise his friends with Christmas cookies to make them happy.

**17. How does paragraph 6 impact the plot of "Jack's First Christmas in Africa"?**

a. It shows that Jack is eager to see how his classmates celebrate Christmas.
b. It compares Jack's Christmas in Africa and his Christmas in America.
c. It describes how Jack's family supports him when he feels homesick.
d. It explains how Christmas traditions have helped Jack make friends at school.

**18. How does the setting of "Jack's First Christmas in Africa" affect the plot of the story?**

a. It creates a situation where Jack has to try new foods and live in a new place.
b. It reveals why Jack has been looking forward to celebrating Christmas in Africa.
c. It shows why Jack's family wanted to move to Africa for missionary work.
d. It makes it difficult for Jack to experience his usual Christmas traditions.

*Refer to BOTH "Little White Lily" and "Jack's First Christmas in Africa" to answer questions 19-21.*

**19. How is the lily in "Little White Lily" similar to Jack in "Jack's First Christmas in Africa"?**

a. Both realize the value of friendship
b. Both were happy to receive something
c. Both were looking forward to a meal
d. Both wanted to receive care from others

**20. What is the main difference between the lily in "Little White Lily" and Jack in "Jack's First Christmas in Africa"?**

a. The lily was expecting the sunshine and rain, but Jack was not expecting the Christmas celebration he received.
b. The lily was happy to receive sunshine and rain, but Jack was not happy about the Christmas surprise.
c. The lily was happy being by herself, but Jack wanted to make friends.
d. The lily was living in an unfamiliar place, but Jack was living in his childhood home.

**21. What theme is found in "Jack's First Christmas in Africa" that is not found in "Little White Lily"?**

a. Being happy to receive something
b. Feeling sad because of lacking something
c. Experiencing the kindness of others
d. Overcoming a challenge through hard work



Copyright © Mometrix Media. You have been licensed one copy of this document for personal use only. Any other reproduction or redistribution is strictly prohibited. All rights reserved.
This content is provided for test preparation purposes only and does not imply an endorsement by Mometrix of any particular political, scientific, or religious point of view.

*Refer to Thomas's First Complaint Letter for questions 22–24.*

**Thomas's First Complaint Letter**

February 24, 2011

Thomas Goodwill

1234 Main Street

Thompson, Texas 77482

Romco Toys

8765 Madison Avenue

New York, New York 10008

To the customer service department:

I bought a Romco talking wind-up doll for my little sister from your website on November 12, 2010. The doll arrived on November 20. My sister opened the box on Christmas Day, and the doll worked fine until three days ago. At that time, my sister noticed that the winding part was getting harder to twist. Now it will not twist at all. The doll no longer talks.

My mom noticed that the papers that came with the doll state that it is guaranteed to work for one year. The papers also state that if the doll stopped working within a year, we should send it back to your company for a replacement. The doll is enclosed in this box. We would like a new doll to replace this one.

Thank you for your time. My sister looks forward to getting a new doll that works.

Sincerely,

Thomas Goodwill

**22. Why did Thomas write this letter?**

a. To invite a friend over for Christmas
b. To replace a doll he bought that broke
c. To buy a wind-up talking doll
d. To ask about a wind-up talking doll

**23. How long is the guarantee for the doll?**

a. One year
b. One month
c. Two years
d. Three months



Copyright © Mometrix Media. You have been licensed one copy of this document for personal use only. Any other reproduction or redistribution is strictly prohibited. All rights reserved.
This content is provided for test preparation purposes only and does not imply an endorsement by Mometrix of any particular political, scientific, or religious point of view.

**24. What does the word "defective" mean?**

a. Ugly
b. Definitive
c. Broken
d. Expensive

*Refer to Romco's Toys Reply Letter for questions 22–24.*

**Romco's Toys Reply Letter**

March 5, 2011

Customer Service Department

Romco Toys

8765 Madison Avenue

New York, New York 10008

Dear Customer:

Romco's wind-up doll was a very popular item with girls this Christmas. Unfortunately, many of the toys sold before the holidays had a defective winding mechanism that gradually became harder to turn. It made it impossible to operate the doll's unique speaking features. This defect is the responsibility of the manufacturers, so we are asking our customers to help the company recoup some of the loss it experienced due to this problem.

Included in this letter is a form we are asking all customers to fill out to receive a replacement doll. The form provides Romco with the documentation necessary to recover money lost from replacing the defective dolls. Please fill out the form and put it in the prepaid envelope provided. Romco will assume all postage costs for the letter and the replacement doll. After the form is received, Romco will send a new doll free of charge. Thank you for your concern in this matter.

Sincerely,

Romco Customer Service Department

**25. What did Romco Toys agree to do for Thomas?**

a. Fix the old doll and return it
b. Give Thomas a coupon to buy a new doll
c. Talk to the manufacturer about the problem
d. Send Thomas a replacement doll

**26. What did Romco Toys ask Thomas to do?**

a. Operate the doll's unique speaking features
b. Fill out a form and send it to Romco Toys
c. Write to the manufacturers about the problem
d. Buy a new doll



Copyright © Mometrix Media. You have been licensed one copy of this document for personal use only. Any other reproduction or redistribution is strictly prohibited. All rights reserved.
This content is provided for test preparation purposes only and does not imply an endorsement by Mometrix of any particular political, scientific, or religious point of view.

**27. The following are four statements about the Romco doll.**

9. Thomas purchased the doll on November 12, 2011.
10. The doll worked on Christmas Day.
11. The doll had a pretty voice.
12. The doll stopped working in February.

Which of these statements is an opinion about the doll?

a. Statement 1
b. Statement 2
c. Statement 3
d. Statement 4

*Refer to both Thomas's First Complaint Letter and Romco's Toys Reply Letter for questions 28–31.*

**28. According to both letters, what is the correct format for writing the name of a town and state in an address?**

a. Anywhere Texas
b. Anywhere, Texas
c. Anywhere Texas
d. Anywhere, Texas

**29. Why did Romco Toys call Thomas "Customer" in its letter?**

a. Romco Toys had so many complaints it couldn't write individual letters
b. Thomas did not write his name in his letter
c. In the letter, Romco Toys said it is standard procedure to not use customers' names
d. Thomas was not a customer; his sister received the doll

**30. How long did it take Romco Toys to reply to Thomas's letter?**

a. Two weeks
b. Two months
c. Nine weeks
d. Nine days

**31. Tone in writing describes the feelings or impressions a piece of writing give the reader. Just a few examples of tone are happy, sad, polite, and angry. Which of the following best describes the tone of both letters?**

a. Angry
b. Polite
c. Silly
d. Rude



Copyright © Mometrix Media. You have been licensed one copy of this document for personal use only. Any other reproduction or redistribution is strictly prohibited. All rights reserved.
This content is provided for test preparation purposes only and does not imply an endorsement by Mometrix of any particular political, scientific, or religious point of view.

*Refer to the following for questions 32–40.*

**The Joy of Jump Rope**

(1) There are many types of sports and physical activities across the world. Some types require having a team of people or special training and equipment. However, jumping rope only requires a rope, does not need other people, and is a simple and fun way to exercise.

(2) You may have jumped rope as part of gym class or when playing with friends. History tells us that people have been jumping rope for thousands of years, and ancient people used vines for their jump ropes. Eventually, jump rope spread to other countries and started to become popular because it could be done in small spaces and was not expensive. People jumping rope began to come up with creative rhymes that could be said or sung in time with the skip of the rope. They also came up with different jumping techniques to make it even more fun and interesting.

(3) In fact, jumping rope has become a competitive sport over the past years. In competitions, athletes do as many jumps as possible in a time limit or showcase routines made up of different jumping skills. The most advanced athletes can do splits, handstands, and even backflips in their jump rope routines!

(4) Although you can jump rope without other people, there are ways to get friends or family involved with jumping rope too. With three people and a long rope, two people can turn the rope and one person can jump in the middle. Double Dutch is another type of jump rope that can be done with two turners and one jumper, except two ropes are used and turned in an alternating pattern. Or, you might decide to make up your own creative rhymes and routines together.

(5) Jumping rope isn't just fun, it also has many benefits for our health. When you jump rope, your heart pumps faster. Your heart is a muscle, like the muscles of our arms and legs. So, making the heart work a little harder through jumping rope helps the heart become stronger. Speaking of muscles in the arms and legs, jump rope also strengthens them since you need to use them continuously to keep the rope turning.

(6) Our bones also benefit from jumping rope. When we place small amounts of stress on our bones, like through repeated jumping, the bones respond to that stress and build themselves up to become even stronger. Over time, jumping rope will feel easier and less tiring as you gain heart, muscle, and bone strength.



Copyright © Mometrix Media. You have been licensed one copy of this document for personal use only. Any other reproduction or redistribution is strictly prohibited. All rights reserved.
This content is provided for test preparation purposes only and does not imply an endorsement by Mometrix of any particular political, scientific, or religious point of view.

**32. What can the reader infer based on the information in paragraph 3?**

a. Getting started with jumping rope is time consuming.
b. Only athletes benefit from jumping rope.
c. Jump rope skills can be improved with practice.
d. You need a special type of rope to jump rope successfully.

**33. Which of the following is most likely the author's reason for including the information in paragraph 4?**

a. To describe different ways of jumping rope
b. To show the events that led to the creation of jump rope
c. To prove that jump rope can be more fun than other activities
d. To describe the process of getting started with jumping rope

**34. The passage "The Joy of Jump Rope" uses an organizational structure that:**

a. Presents a narrative about people that have enjoyed jump rope
b. Describes the effects of becoming a competitive jump rope athlete
c. Highlights how jumping rope can be fun and improve health and fitness
d. Explains how jumping rope has become one of the most popular activities

**35. Which of the following details belongs in a summary of "The Joy of Jump Rope"?**

a. Jumping rope started with people using vines during ancient times.
b. Jumping rope is inexpensive since it only requires a rope.
c. Jumping rope is better than other activities because it is less likely to injure someone.
d. Jumping rope is fun and can improve health and fitness in multiple ways.

**36. Paragraphs 5 and 6 support which of the following key ideas?**

a. Jumping rope too often can lead to injury.
b. Jump rope is one of the best ways to become healthier.
c. The body can adapt and get more fit over time through jump rope.
d. Jumping rope can be done by yourself or with others.

**37. Based on the passage, what conclusion can the reader make about jumping rope?**

a. Jumping rope costs less than many other sports or activities.
b. Jumping rope is one of the most popular activities worldwide.
c. Double Dutch is much more difficult than jumping over a single rope.
d. Jumping rope is more effective than running for improving fitness.

**38. Which sentence from the passage explains how jumping rope first began?**

a. There are many types of sports and physical activities across the world.
b. History tells us that people have been jumping rope for thousands of years, and ancient people used vines for their jump ropes.
c. In fact, jumping rope has become a competitive sport over the past years.
d. Although you can jump without other people, there are ways to get friends or family involved with jumping rope too.



Copyright © Mometrix Media. You have been licensed one copy of this document for personal use only. Any other reproduction or redistribution is strictly prohibited. All rights reserved.
This content is provided for test preparation purposes only and does not imply an endorsement by Mometrix of any particular political, scientific, or religious point of view.

**39. How do paragraphs 5 and 6 help the reader understand the health benefits of jumping rope?**

a. By comparing and contrasting jump rope with other activities
b. By explaining which parts of the body benefit from jumping rope
c. By identifying different ways to jump rope with friends and family
d. By ranking the results of jumping rope from most to least important

**40. With which of the following would the author most likely agree?**

a. Jump rope is the most competitive sport in the world.
b. Jump rope is mostly beneficial as a mental exercise.
c. Jump rope is an easy activity for people to engage in almost anywhere.
d. Jump rope is an activity that has grown in popularity only recently.



Copyright © Mometrix Media. You have been licensed one copy of this document for personal use only. Any other reproduction or redistribution is strictly prohibited. All rights reserved.
This content is provided for test preparation purposes only and does not imply an endorsement by Mometrix of any particular political, scientific, or religious point of view.

# Answer Key and Explanations for Test #1

**1. D:** The main objective of these paragraphs is to describe Manolo's and Barry's neighborhood.

**2. A:** The strange thing about the name of Barry's and Manolo's neighborhood is that there are no Cypress trees and the land is flat.

**3. A:** The first sentence shows that Cypress Heights residents do everything in their control (painting their houses and decorating their lawns) to make their places look nice.

**4. A:** Barry and Manolo like living close to each other because it makes it convenient for them to visit each other.

**5. B:** The boys met Mrs. Juarez, who had just moved in.

**6. C:** Plants that can live in very dry climates are called drought-resistant.

**7. D:** Mrs. Juarez put gravel on her lawn instead of grass. She used gravel because she wouldn't have to water it.

**8. B:** Traditionally, new neighbors receive gifts, not give them. That is why Barry asked Mrs. Juarez that question.

**9. A:** Knit in this case means to join together tightly.

**10. C:** While Mrs. Juarez may turn out to be a good friend, the main lesson she taught Barry and Manolo is that with the right plants, gardens can grow anywhere.

**11. C:** The poem says that the little white lily droops as it waits for the sunshine and droops in pain as it waits for rain. Once the lily has received both sunshine and rain, the lily "is happy again." While the lily in the poem is sitting by a stone, the poem does not support the idea that all lilies grow by stones. This makes choice A incorrect. The lily receives sunshine before it receives rain. However, the Sun came back out, so the rain did not occur in the evening. Choice B is not supported by the poem, so it is incorrect. The lily in the poem is described as white. However, the poem does not contain information that shows that all lilies are white, so choice D is incorrect.

**12. D:** The simile "dressed like a bride" is used to compare the white petals of the lily to a white wedding dress. This comparison helps the reader imagine the color and shape of the lily. Some of the lily's emotions are described in the poem. However, the poem does not include details that show that the lily is excited or nervous, so choice A is incorrect. The poem does not mention people celebrating the lily, so choice B is incorrect. The simile does not provide specific details, such as the number of layers the lily's petals create, so choice C is incorrect.

**13. B:** In lines 25 through 40, the lily is thankful for the sunshine and rain after waiting for them. The poet uses specific words to show this. For example, the lily says that the rain makes her "stronger" and "cool" so that she will not burn in the sunlight. In the last stanza, the poet says that "thanks to the sunshine" and "thanks to the rain," the lily is "happy again." This creates a thankful voice, so choice B is correct. These lines do not create a depressed voice because the events being described and the words that are used are positive, so choice A is incorrect. The poem does not attempt to persuade the reader or argue a point, so choice C is incorrect. In lines 25 through 40, the lily is enjoying being saved from a lack of sunshine and rain, which was hurting her. The words used



Copyright © Mometrix Media. You have been licensed one copy of this document for personal use only. Any other reproduction or redistribution is strictly prohibited. All rights reserved.
This content is provided for test preparation purposes only and does not imply an endorsement by Mometrix of any particular political, scientific, or religious point of view.

in these lines show that she is happy and thankful because she is no longer in pain. She is not being silly, so choice D is incorrect.

**14. C:** In paragraph 15, the presents under the tree for Jack are wrapped in paper that is red and green, "with accents of gold and silver." This description shows that the accents must be things that are added to the red and green paper. Definition 3 describes the way that the gold and silver were used as part of the design of the wrapping paper, so choice C is correct. The word *accent* is not used to describe a way of speaking in the passage, so choice A is incorrect. The author does not use the word *accent* when describing music, so choice B is incorrect. The author does not use the word *accent* when describing a character's concern or attention, so choice D is incorrect.

**15. C:** Paragraph 20 shows that Jack has changed his mind about spending Christmas in Africa by the end of the story. He is likely to use his gift, as he is grateful for it and was surprised by the kindness of his classmates. Jack is not likely to ask his mother to bake her special cookies. Paragraph 6 says that there is no way to get the ingredients used to make them, so choice A is incorrect. Jack is not likely to dread Christmas morning in Africa. His classmates have worked hard to cheer him up and help him enjoy being in Africa for Christmas, so choice B is incorrect. The reader can infer that Jack is grateful for the unexpected kindness of his classmates, so Jack is not likely to refuse to eat the cookies his classmates made for him. Choice D is incorrect.

**16. A:** In line 13, Jack tells his classmates that Christmas is about giving and spending time with friends and family. The end of the story shows Jack that the kindness of his friends is more valuable than participating in the Christmas traditions he is used to. These ideas support choice A, so it is the correct answer. The passage points out that Jack and his classmates have "very different traditions," so choice B is incorrect. The passage does not show that Jack wants to help his family adjust to living in Africa. The passage only describes how Jack feels about living in Africa, so choice C is incorrect. Jack does not plan a surprise for his classmates. Instead, Jack's classmates surprise him for Christmas, so choice D is incorrect.

**17. B:** Paragraph 6 lists the things Jack does not have to celebrate Christmas in Africa that he is used to having in America. This contrast is important to the plot because it shows that Jack does not expect to experience any of his American traditions in Africa. This is the main conflict of the story. The conflict is resolved when Jack's classmates surprise him by recreating the traditions he is used to. Choice B is correct. Paragraph 6 shows what Jack misses about Christmas in America. It does not show that he is eager to see African Christmas traditions, so choice A is incorrect. Paragraph 6 does not describe how Jack's family supports him, so choice C is incorrect. Paragraph 6 does not explain how Jack made friends at school, so choice D is incorrect.

**18. D:** The story is set in Africa. Jack is from America, where he got to participate in Christmas traditions that he loved. Africa and America are very different, and the differences make it hard for Jack to participate in the Christmas traditions he enjoys. The passage does show that Jack has gotten used to the food in Africa and their new home. However, these details are not what creates the conflict in the story, so choice A is incorrect. The passage explains that Jack is dreading celebrating Christmas in Africa. He is not looking forward to celebrating it, so choice B is incorrect. Jack's parents' desire to be missionaries explains why the story is set in Africa. However, this reason does not affect the plot of the story, so choice C is incorrect.

**19. B:** Both the lily and Jack were happy to receive something. In "Little White Lily," the lily was waiting for sunshine and rain. When the lily received them, she said it was "good," and they made the lily "happy again." In "Jack's First Christmas in Africa," Jack was happy to receive a surprise from his classmates, who recreated some of his American Christmas traditions. While Jack realized the



Copyright © Mometrix Media. You have been licensed one copy of this document for personal use only. Any other reproduction or redistribution is strictly prohibited. All rights reserved.
This content is provided for test preparation purposes only and does not imply an endorsement by Mometrix of any particular political, scientific, or religious point of view.

value of friendship with his classmates, the lily does not experience friendship, so choice A is incorrect. While the lily was waiting for sunshine as "clothing and food," "Jack's First Christmas in Africa" does not state that Jack was looking forward to a meal. In fact, Jack was dreading the days leading up to Christmas because food like his mom's special Christmas cookies wouldn't be part of the holiday, so choice C is incorrect. While Jack receives care from his classmates, the lily does not receive care from another character. Additionally, Jack was not hoping that his classmates would do something to care for him, so choice D is incorrect.

**20. A:** In "Little White Lily," the lily is described as waiting "till the sun shone" and "waiting for the wet rain." Jack's Christmas celebration with his African classmates was a surprise, so it was not something he was waiting for. Both Jack and the lily were happy about what they received, so choice B is incorrect. The poem does not say that the lily was happy being by herself. The story also does not say that Jack wanted to make friends. In fact, "Jack's First Christmas in Africa" says that Jack had made friends, so choice C is incorrect. Jack was the one living in an unfamiliar place, not the lily, so choice D is incorrect.

**21. C:** Jack experiences the kindness of others when his classmates surprise him. However, the lily receives what she needs from nature, not from others being kind. Both Jack and the lily were happy to receive something, so choice A is incorrect. In the poem, the lily was "drooping" when waiting for the sunshine and rain, and in the story, Jack was sad to miss out on his Christmas traditions. Both characters were sad that they were missing something, so choice B is incorrect. Neither Jack nor the lily overcame a challenge through hard work, so choice D is incorrect.

**22. B:** Thomas wanted to replace a doll he bought for his sister, which broke before the warranty was up.

**23. A:** The warranty or guarantee for the doll was for one year.

**24. C:** The word "defective" is another way of saying "broken."

**25. D:** The company agreed to send Thomas a replacement doll after he sent in some paperwork.

**26. B:** Romco asked Thomas to fill out a form and send it to them.

**27. C:** This sentence is an opinion about an aspect of the doll. It can be debated. Not everyone would agree it is a fact.

**28. D:** The correct form for writing the name of a town and state is Anywhere, Texas.

**29. A:** Romco did not have time to write an individual letter to all of the customers with complaints, so they wrote a general letter to all people who complained.

**30. D:** It took nine days for Romco to reply to Thomas's letter according to the dates on the letters.

**31. B:** The tone in both letters is polite.

**32. C:** Paragraph 3 explains that jump rope has become a competitive sport, and advanced athletes can complete movements that require a high level of skill. The reader can infer that athletes develop these skills through practicing and improving their jump rope skills, so choice C is correct. The statements in the paragraph do not claim that getting started with jumping rope is time consuming, so choice A is incorrect. While paragraph 3 mentions athletes, it does not suggest that only athletes benefit from jumping rope, so choice B is incorrect. No type of rope is described in paragraph 3, so choice D is incorrect.



Copyright © Mometrix Media. You have been licensed one copy of this document for personal use only. Any other reproduction or redistribution is strictly prohibited. All rights reserved.
This content is provided for test preparation purposes only and does not imply an endorsement by Mometrix of any particular political, scientific, or religious point of view.

**33. A:** Paragraph 4 states that jumping rope can be done with other people by using two ropes instead of one or by practicing rhymes and routines, so choice B is correct. Paragraph 4 does not explain jump rope's beginnings, so choice B is incorrect. Jump rope's beginnings are described in paragraph 2. The author does not use paragraph 4 to attempt to prove to the reader that jumping rope can be more fun than other activities, so choice C is incorrect. Paragraph 4 lists ways to jump rope but does not explain how to start jumping rope, so choice D is incorrect.

**34. C:** The passage suggests that jumping rope can be fun by explaining that it can be done with friends and family, that it can involve elements like routines and flips, and that it can be done competitively. The passage also explains how jumping rope can improve health and fitness by listing the specific body parts that it can strengthen. These elements in the passage make choice C correct. The passage does not tell a narrative about people who jump rope, so choice A is incorrect. The passage mentions that jumping rope has become a competitive sport that athletes compete in. However, it does not provide the effects of becoming a competitive jump rope athlete, so choice B is incorrect. While the passage does explain how jumping rope began and spread, this is a supporting detail. It is not discussed throughout the passage, so choice D is incorrect.

**35. D:** The detail in choice D is correct because it restates the central idea of the passage. Because it would help a reader understand what the passage is about, choice D would be appropriate to include in a summary. The passage does describe jump rope's beginnings. However, the fact that people used to use vines instead of ropes is a small detail. It does not belong in a summary of the passage because it is not one of the passage's key ideas, so choice A is incorrect. Choice B is incorrect because it is also a small detail. The fact that jump rope is an easy activity to get into is a main idea of the passage. However, the fact that it only requires a rope is only a supporting detail. Choice C makes a claim that is not found in the passage, so it is incorrect.

**36. C:** Paragraphs 5 and 6 explain that jumping rope works the heart, muscles, and bones and that each of these parts of the body can become stronger over time if a person continues jumping rope, so choice C is correct. Paragraphs 5 and 6 do not suggest that jumping rope too often can lead to injury, so choice A is incorrect. Paragraphs 5 and 6 explain the health benefits of jump rope, but they do not claim that jumping rope is one of the best ways to get healthier, so choice B is incorrect. The idea that jump rope can be done alone or with others is supported by paragraph 4, not paragraphs 5 and 6, so choice D is incorrect.

**37. A:** The passage explains that the only equipment needed to jump rope is a rope. This fact supports the conclusion that jumping rope costs less than many other types of sports or activities. Other sports require many pieces of equipment. For example, hockey requires skates, a hockey stick, pads, and a helmet. Therefore, choice A is correct. The passage does not discuss the popularity of jump rope around the world, so choice B is incorrect. The passage does mention Double Dutch. However, it does not compare the difficulty of Double Dutch to the difficulty of jumping over a single rope, so choice C is incorrect. The passage does not compare the health benefits of jump rope to the health benefits of running or any other fitness activities, so choice D is incorrect.

**38. B:** The sentence in choice B tells the reader that jumping rope began with ancient people using vines for jump ropes, so it is correct. The sentence in choice A does not discuss jumping rope, so it is incorrect. The sentence in choice C explains that jump rope has grown over the years, but is does not explain how it first began, so it is also incorrect. The sentence in choice D is incorrect because it claims that a person can jump rope alone or with others. It does not tell the reader how the activity first began.



Copyright © Mometrix Media. You have been licensed one copy of this document for personal use only. Any other reproduction or redistribution is strictly prohibited. All rights reserved.
This content is provided for test preparation purposes only and does not imply an endorsement by Mometrix of any particular political, scientific, or religious point of view.

**39. B:** Paragraphs 5 and 6 help the reader understand the health benefits of jumping rope by explaining which parts of the body, such as the heart, muscles, and bones, can get stronger when a person jumps rope, so choice B is correct. Paragraphs 5 and 6 do not compare and contrast jumping rope to other activities, so choice A is incorrect. Paragraphs 5 and 6 do not list different ways to jump rope, so choice C is incorrect. The information in paragraphs 5 and 6 is not given in order of importance, so choice D is incorrect.

**40. C:** Jump rope is an easy activity for people to engage in almost anywhere. The first paragraph of the passage says that a person only needs a rope and can even do jump rope alone. Even though the author states that jump rope is a competitive sport, it is not compared to other activities. Choice B is wrong because the author never talks about the mental benefit of jumprope. While jump rope does require attention and likely acts as a good mental exercise, it is even more clear that it is a good activity for the heart, bones, and muscles. Choice D is not implied by the passage. The author talks about how jump rope has been popular for thousands of years.



Copyright © Mometrix Media. You have been licensed one copy of this document for personal use only. Any other reproduction or redistribution is strictly prohibited. All rights reserved.
This content is provided for test preparation purposes only and does not imply an endorsement by Mometrix of any particular political, scientific, or religious point of view.

# Practice Test #2

*Refer to the following for questions 1–9:*

**Hobie's Journey Across the Finish Line**

(1) "On your marks, get set, GO!"

(2) While the crack of the starting gun was still ringing in his ears, Hobie straightened his right leg so fast he felt a twinge in his knee. He then swung his left leg straight in front of him. When he looked up, he was surprised to find himself nearly halfway up the track. His heart was thumping hard and fast in his chest.

(3) "Go easy," Hobie thought. "You have three-and-a-half more laps to go."
He took a deep breath and lifted his legs slightly to relax his stride. His shoulders dropped a little as he swung his arms. Hobie's chest felt a little less tight. His feet tapped the track as Hobie matched the sound of his footfalls to those of the runners behind him.

(4) "Try to save some steam for the end," said Coach Bennett. "That's when you can catch up to the jack rabbits that used up everything in the first lap."

(5) Hobie loved going fast for as long as he could remember. In kindergarten, he was always first to cross the finish line during running races at recess. He won an award in second grade for running the fastest mile in gym. But every spring, Hobie chose playing baseball over track, despite his parent's pleas to consider track.

(6) "You're such a good runner," said his mother. "And it would be so much easier because we would only have to drive to one practice."

(7) Hobie's older brother, Martin, was a member of the county's local track club. Martin had joined seven years earlier and was now one of the team's star sprinters. But Hobie did not want to be compared to his brother on the track. Few people in the town's Little League association even knew that Hobie had a brother, much less a brother who could run 100 meters in less than 15 seconds. Hobie wasn't the strongest player on his baseball team. He didn't like spending so much time on the bench, but he loved how he was always called "Hobie" or "Hobie Smith," never "Martin's little brother."

(8) Three months ago, in March, Hobie was all set for his fifth year in Little League. He had been practicing throwing and batting after school. His aim was improving, and so was his throwing speed. Hobie hoped his efforts would mean he would spend more time in his position, right outfield, and less time on the bench. Then Hobie and Martin's father had an accident at work. Mr. Smith fell from a ladder and broke his leg and arm. He could not work or drive for six months.



Copyright © Mometrix Media. You have been licensed one copy of this document for personal use only. Any other reproduction or redistribution is strictly prohibited. All rights reserved.
This content is provided for test preparation purposes only and does not imply an endorsement by Mometrix of any particular political, scientific, or religious point of view.

(9) "I don't have time to get home from work and drive to two different practices," said Hobie's mother, Mrs. Smith, to Hobie. "And it's not fair to make Martin switch to baseball after he's been in track for seven years and is doing so well. I'm sorry Hobie, but you have only one choice for a sport this spring, and it's track. You don't have to join, but if you don't, you're staying home with Dad."

(10) Luckily, the coach for Hobie's track team, Coach Bennett, was new. He didn't know Hobie even had a brother. Also, Hobie turned out to be better at long distances. Coach Bennett had him focus on the mile and the 800-meters events. At the last meet, Hobie ran a mile in just under seven minutes.

(11) "You keep that up, and I'm kidnapping you for the high school cross-country running team in the fall!" Coach Bennett joked after the race.

(12) Hobie was now finishing his first turn with only two other runners ahead of him. He couldn't believe how well he had done this season. In baseball, Hobie always struggled to pay attention in the field. He loved batting, running bases, and catching fly balls, but hated the endless hours of waiting out in the field or on the bench for something to happen. In track, he was always moving. And, for the first time, he was doing very well. He was the fastest distance runner on his team, and had won three out of the seven races he ran that season. Hobie pushed his legs a bit faster and caught up to the second-place runner. There was just one person blocking his view of the finish line.

(13) Hobie felt his legs fly through the air and his chest start to hurt a little. He puffed his cheeks and swung his arms hard. Two more laps to go. Hobie kept pace a few feet behind the runner in the lead until they rounded the last bend of the track. Hobie drew a deep, ragged breath and started to run a little faster, making the distance between him and the other runner a few feet shorter. Hobie kept sprinting until he was running side by side with the runner in the lead. The finish line came into view. With his last ounce of strength, Hobie pushed past the other runner and swung his arms as hard as he could, flying over the finish line four yards ahead of the other runner.

(14) "Good job!" shouted Coach Bennett, rushing out to jog alongside him. Hobie slowed down and leaned over to catch his breath, placing his hands on his knees. Then he looked up into the stands and saw his father waving his good arm. Hobie waved back. He was no longer angry that he couldn't play baseball. He was glad to be running track.

**1. Why did Hobie choose baseball instead of track?**

a. Hobie's parents wanted him to play baseball
b. Hobie wanted to avoid being compared to his older brother
c. Hobie was a better baseball player than runner
d. Hobie's brother, Martin, also played baseball



Copyright © Mometrix Media. You have been licensed one copy of this document for personal use only. Any other reproduction or redistribution is strictly prohibited. All rights reserved.
This content is provided for test preparation purposes only and does not imply an endorsement by Mometrix of any particular political, scientific, or religious point of view.

**2. In paragraph 2, what does the word "twinge" mean?**

a. Hurt
b. Bend
c. Break
d. Loosen

**3. Which sentence from paragraphs 5 and 6 shows that Hobie is a good runner?**

a. "Hobie wasn't the strongest player on his baseball team"
b. "Hobie loved going fast for as long as he could remember"
c. "But Hobie did not want to be compared to his brother on the track"
d. "In kindergarten, he was always first to cross the finish line during running races at recess"

**4.**

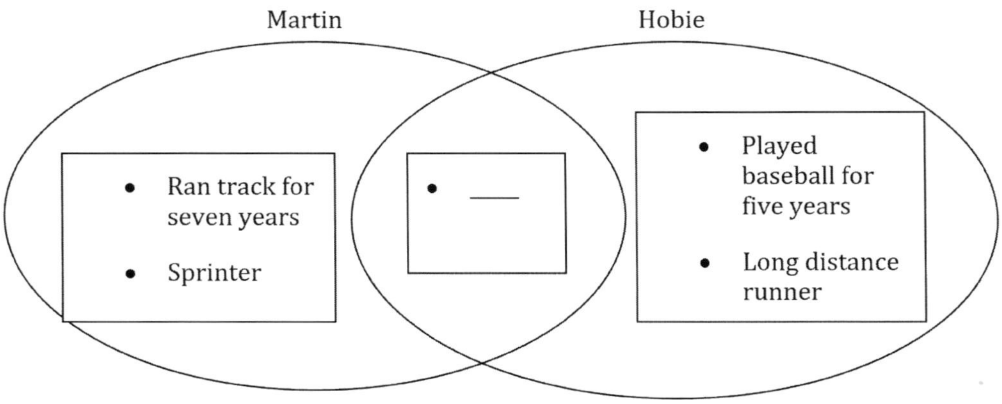


**Which of the following phrases belongs in the blank?**

a. Good at running
b. Older brother
c. Younger brother
d. Ran on high school cross-country team

**5. What is the most likely lesson a reader will learn from this story?**

a. Track is a better sport than baseball
b. It is dangerous to use ladders
c. Hard decisions can have positive outcomes
d. Big brothers like to be compared to little brothers

**6. Increased tension or excitement in a story is called suspense. How does the author build suspense in the story "Hobie's Journey across the Finish Line"?**

a. By describing how Hobie's father hurt himself at work
b. By describing how Hobie got better at running long distances
c. By showing why Hobie had to switch to track from baseball
d. By describing how Hobie got from third to first place in the race



Copyright © Mometrix Media. You have been licensed one copy of this document for personal use only. Any other reproduction or redistribution is strictly prohibited. All rights reserved.
This content is provided for test preparation purposes only and does not imply an endorsement by Mometrix of any particular political, scientific, or religious point of view.

**7. Which choice is the best summary of this story?**

a. Despite showing a talent for running, Hobie chose to play baseball to avoid comparisons to his older brother. His father's accident forced him to join track, where he did well
b. Hobie disliked his older brother and decided to get back at him by joining baseball instead of track. Hobie later joined track to show his brother, Martin, that he is a better runner
c. Hobie wasn't very good at baseball, so he practiced throwing, catching, and hitting every day after school until he got better
d. A boy loved to run, but chose to play baseball instead. Later, he switched to track

**8. What is the best definition of the word "ragged" as it is used in paragraph 13?**

a. Roughly kept
b. Having a torn edge or outline
c. Worn-out from stress and strain
d. Wearing tattered clothes

**9. Based on the events of this story, what is Hobie most likely to do next year?**

a. Join track as a sprinter to compete against his brother
b. Join Little League and compete to be a pitcher
c. Join track as a long distance runner
d. Join Little League and play right field

*Refer to the following for questions 10–15:*

**My Shadow**

by Robert Louis Stevenson

I have a little shadow that goes in and out with me,
And what can be the use of him is more than I can see.
He is very, very like me from the heels up to the head;
And I see him jump before me, when I jump into my bed.
The funniest thing about him is the way he likes to grow—
Not at all like proper children, which is always very slow;
For he sometimes shoots up taller like an India-rubber ball,
And he sometimes gets so little that there's none of him at all.
He hasn't got a notion of how children ought to play,
And can only make a fool of me in every sort of way.
He stays so close beside me, he's a coward, you can see;
I'd think shame to stick to nursie as that shadow sticks to me!
One morning, very early, before the sun was up,
I rose and found the shining dew on every buttercup;
But my lazy little shadow, like an errant sleepy-head,
Had stayed at home behind me and was fast asleep in bed.

**10. Lines 5 through 8 support the key idea that:**

a. The shadow is purposely teasing the speaker.
b. The speaker's shadow can only be seen during the day.
c. The speaker thinks that his shadow is being silly.
d. The speaker's shadow is not always the same size as the speaker.



Copyright © Mometrix Media. You have been licensed one copy of this document for personal use only. Any other reproduction or redistribution is strictly prohibited. All rights reserved.
This content is provided for test preparation purposes only and does not imply an endorsement by Mometrix of any particular political, scientific, or religious point of view.

**11. The author's use of personification in lines 9 through 12 of "My Shadow" helps demonstrate that:**

a. The shadow does not like the speaker.
b. The shadow is able to speak.
c. The shadow seems to have a mind of its own.
d. The shadow is a trickster.

**12. Based on the speaker's descriptions in the poem, which two statements describe how the speaker thinks of his shadow? Select all that may apply.**

a. The speaker hopes that he and his shadow can be friends.
b. The speaker does not understand the behavior of his shadow.
c. The speaker worries that his shadow is lonely.
d. The speaker is afraid of his shadow.
e. The speaker believes the shadow has negative qualities.

**13. Which sentence from the poem shows that the shadow moves with the speaker?**

a. He hasn't got a notion of how children ought to play
b. Had stayed at home behind me and was fast asleep in bed
c. For he sometimes shoots up taller like an India-rubber ball
d. And I see him jump before me, when I jump into my bed

**14. The author says his shadow is "like an India-rubber ball," which is similar to a bouncy ball. With that knowledge, what is most likely the reason the author used the simile "like an India-rubber ball" to describe his shadow?**

a. To show how suddenly the shadow's height can increase
b. To show that the shadow is round, like a ball
c. To show that the speaker wants the shadow to play with him
d. To show that the shadow can be tinier than a toy ball

**15. Based on lines 13 through 16, what can the reader conclude about the speaker's shadow?**

a. The speaker's shadow can be seen at any time of day.
b. The speaker's shadow stayed home because he was upset.
c. The speaker's shadow cannot be seen when there is no light.
d. The speaker's shadow has become boring to him.

*Refer to the following for questions 16–24:*

**Sticky Water**

(1) News flash: water is sticky. This is a surprise to many people because water does not seem sticky. In fact, it's the first thing that people reach for to wash away stickiness and any other kind of dirt. The second item, of course, is soap.

(2) Water and things like glue are sticky in different ways. Glue is sticky in two ways. Water is sticky in only one way. Glue feels and acts sticky. It is used to join objects such as paper, wood, and plastic together. Water does not feel or act sticky.

(3) Glue is sticky in two ways. One way is called adhesion. This is when glue, after it is poured on a surface, spreads into tiny holes and dents and hardens. The glue holds the surfaces together like the pieces of a jigsaw puzzle. However, for glue to work well, it also needs to stick to itself and hold together. This is called cohesion.



Copyright © Mometrix Media. You have been licensed one copy of this document for personal use only. Any other reproduction or redistribution is strictly prohibited. All rights reserved.
This content is provided for test preparation purposes only and does not imply an endorsement by Mometrix of any particular political, scientific, or religious point of view.

(4) Water does not have adhesion. If you pour it on a piece of wood, the wood will absorb the water, but water will not harden to make two things stick together. Water does have cohesion. Water is a unique substance made up of two elements: hydrogen (H) and oxygen (O). Water is made up of two parts hydrogen and one part oxygen. The formula for water is H2O. The hydrogen atoms not only stick to the oxygen, but also to other water molecules, much in the same way magnets stick to metal. Water molecules stick to each other because of "hydrogen bonds." If water did not hold together, it could not be a liquid. It would boil and turn into steam.

(5) To see the "stickiness" of water, try the following experiment. This experiment is not dangerous, and it only requires ordinary objects that you probably have at home. However, you will end up spilling some water, so ask an adult if it is okay to do the experiment before starting.

**STICKY WATER Experiment**

You will need the following for this experiment:

- One short plastic cup
- One small pitcher of water
- At least 20 pennies
- A sponge or rag for spills

1. First, fill the plastic cup with water from the pitcher. Make sure to fill the cup all the way up to the rim. Don't spill any water! If you spill water, wipe it up. Make sure the very full glass is sitting on a dry spot.
2. Next, carefully slip a penny into the cup and look closely. Did any of the water spill over the edge? Probably not. Continue adding pennies slowly to avoid splashing. Slip them in gently. Do not throw them in.
3. Keep putting in pennies until water spills over the edge.

How many pennies did it take for the water to spill over? It was probably more than you thought. Most people who do this experiment think one or two pennies will make the very full glass spill, but usually it takes more than 10 pennies. The explanation for this is cohesion. Each time you put in a penny, the water molecules hold on tighter and tighter to each other. Finally, when there is absolutely no more room in the glass and they're hanging over the edge of the glass, the water spills. One time, a scientist was able to get 25 pennies into the glass before it spilled! Now that's sticky water!

**16. What does the word *absorb* mean, as used in paragraph 4?**

a. To soak up
b. To become darker
c. To push away
d. To make sticky



Copyright © Mometrix Media. You have been licensed one copy of this document for personal use only. Any other reproduction or redistribution is strictly prohibited. All rights reserved.
This content is provided for test preparation purposes only and does not imply an endorsement by Mometrix of any particular political, scientific, or religious point of view.

**17. Which sentence from the passage best demonstrates that water performs differently than glue?**

a. If you pour it on a piece of wood, the wood will absorb the water, but the water will not harden to make things stick together.
b. Finally, when there is absolutely no more room in the glass and they're hanging over the edge of the glass, the water spills.
c. The hydrogen atoms not only stick to the oxygen, but also to other water molecules, much in the same way magnets stick to metal.
d. Water is a unique substance made up of two elements: hydrogen (H) and oxygen (O).

**18. Which key idea is supported by the information in paragraph 3?**

a. Glue is neither a solid nor a liquid.
b. Water has unique chemical properties.
c. Water is used to clean surfaces.
d. There are multiple ways for a substance to be sticky.

**19. What conclusion can the reader make about the Sticky Water Experiment?**

a. Other liquids besides water would behave in the same way if they were used in the experiment.
b. The same number of pennies will make the water spill each time.
c. Throwing the pennies in might make the water spill sooner.
d. Glue is made of the same elements as water.

**20. What is the central idea of "Sticky Water"?**

a. Not all science experiments are dangerous.
b. Glue is sticky in multiple ways.
c. Water is used to wash away stickiness.
d. Water is sticky in a way people do not expect.

**21. How do paragraphs 3 and 4 help the reader understand the stickiness of water?**

a. By explaining multiple uses for water
b. By describing what to do with water in the experiment
c. By comparing the qualities of glue to the qualities of water
d. By arguing that water is the best things to use when washing sticky things

**22. What is most likely the author's purpose for writing "Sticky Water"?**

a. To provide a sequence of events that resulted in a discovery about water
b. To argue that water is the most unique substance
c. To explain the sticky qualities of water due to cohesion
d. To suggest that the reader try other experiments involving water

**23. What can the reader infer based on the section "Sticky Water Experiment"?**

a. Adding pennies to a cup of glue will cause the glue to spill.
b. The experiment could also be done with other small objects.
c. The stickiness of water can be shown through many experiments.
d. Adhesion and cohesion are different names for the same thing.



Copyright © Mometrix Media. You have been licensed one copy of this document for personal use only. Any other reproduction or redistribution is strictly prohibited. All rights reserved.
This content is provided for test preparation purposes only and does not imply an endorsement by Mometrix of any particular political, scientific, or religious point of view.

**24. How does the bulleted list under "Sticky Water Experiment" help the reader understand the experiment?**

a. It provides the reader with step-by-step instructions.
b. It gives the reader the list of items needed for the experiment.
c. It uses similes that help the reader imagine what water molecules look like.
d. It shows the reader that the experiment is easy and safe to complete at home.

*Refer to the following for questions 25–27:*

**Chapter 1 My Early Home**

by Anna Sewell

(An excerpt from *Black Beauty: The Autobiography of a Horse*)

(1) The first place that I can well remember was a large pleasant meadow with a pond of clear water in it. Some shady trees leaned over it, and rushes and water-lilies grew at the deep end. Over the hedge on one side we looked into a plowed field, and on the other we looked over a gate at our master's house, which stood by the roadside; at the top of the meadow was a grove of fir trees, and at the bottom a running brook overhung by a steep bank.

(2) While I was young I lived upon my mother's milk, as I could not eat grass. In the daytime I ran by her side, and at night I lay down close by her. When it was hot we used to stand by the pond in the shade of the trees, and when it was cold we had a nice warm shed near the grove.

(3) As soon as I was old enough to eat grass my mother used to go out to work in the daytime, and come back in the evening.

(4) There were six young colts in the meadow besides me; they were older than I was; some were nearly as large as grown-up horses. I used to run with them, and had great fun; we used to gallop all together round and round the field as hard as we could go. Sometimes we had rather rough play, for they would frequently bite and kick as well as gallop.

(5) One day, when there was a good deal of kicking, my mother whinnied to me to come to her, and then she said:

(6) "I wish you to pay attention to what I am going to say to you. The colts who live here are very good colts, but they are cart-horse colts, and of course they have not learned manners. You have been well-bred and well-born; your father has a great name in these parts, and your grandfather won the cup two years at the Newmarket races; your grandmother had the sweetest temper of any horse I ever knew, and I think you have never seen me kick or bite. I hope you will grow up gentle and good, and never learn bad ways; do your work with a good will, lift your feet up well when you trot, and never bite or kick even in play."

(7) I have never forgotten my mother's advice; I knew she was a wise old horse, and our master thought a great deal of her. Her name was Duchess, but he often called her Pet.



Copyright © Mometrix Media. You have been licensed one copy of this document for personal use only. Any other reproduction or redistribution is strictly prohibited. All rights reserved.
This content is provided for test preparation purposes only and does not imply an endorsement by Mometrix of any particular political, scientific, or religious point of view.

**25. What can the reader infer about the horses discussed in the passage "Chapter 1, My Early Home"?**

a. The horse's mother and father had both won races.
b. The young colts did not like the horse.
c. All the horses that live in the meadow have different jobs.
d. The horse's mother and father like to give advice.

**26. Which sentence best explains how the story's narrator is different from the other colts in the meadow?**

a. While I was young I lived upon my mother's milk, as I could not eat grass.
b. As soon as I was old enough to eat grass my mother used to go out to work in the daytime, and come back in the evening.
c. I used to run with them, and had great fun; we used to gallop all together round and round the field as hard as we could go.
d. The colts who live here are very good colts, but they are cart-horse colts, and of course they have not learned manners.

**27. Why did the author begin the story with a description of the meadow, in paragraph 1?**

a. To explain why the narrator was different from the other colts
b. To illustrate the setting where the narrator grew up
c. To emphasize how the narrator played with the other horses
d. To show that the narrator wanted to live somewhere different



Copyright © Mometrix Media. You have been licensed one copy of this document for personal use only. Any other reproduction or redistribution is strictly prohibited. All rights reserved.
This content is provided for test preparation purposes only and does not imply an endorsement by Mometrix of any particular political, scientific, or religious point of view.

*Refer to the following for questions 28–31:*

**Football Camp**

Cast of Characters:

- Charlie: A fifth-grade boy
- Hayden: A fifth-grade boy
- Jordan: A college football player
- Mr. Thornton: The football camp director

SCENE 1

[*The front porch of* CHARLIE'S *house.* CHARLIE *and* HAYDEN *are sitting on a porch swing and eating sandwiches.* CHARLIE *is swinging his feet and looking around.* HAYDEN *is mostly sitting still.*]

CHARLIE: I can't wait to get up and go to football camp tomorrow! I've been practicing with my brother all week.

[HAYDEN *nods and takes another bite of his sandwich.*]

CHARLIE: We're gonna be pros by Saturday! We're definitely gonna make the team next year. Aren't you excited?

HAYDEN: Yeah, I guess so.

CHARLIE: What do you mean? You seemed really excited about it last week.

HAYDEN: I know. I was! But, now I'm kinda nervous.

CHARLIE: Why? You're awesome at football! You're always one of the first kids picked at recess! I always want you on my team!

HAYDEN: I know, but this week the coaches are football players from a college team! They're so much older and bigger than us! What if they actually tackle us? We'll be crushed!

CHARLIE: Oh, I didn't think about that. You really think they'll be that much bigger than us?

HAYDEN: One day, my parents took me to a college game. We walked into the stadium at the same time as the football players, and they were three times as tall as me!

[CHARLIE lowers his eyebrows and squints.]

CHARLIE: No way! They can't be that tall. They don't look that tall when I watch games on TV!

HAYDEN: Well, that's just because they're so far away from the camera.

[*Both boys pause and take a bite of their sandwiches.*]

CHARLIE: I'm still excited. I think it will be fun either way!

SCENE 2

[*The football field at a local university, in the morning. Four groups of kids are standing around the field.* CHARLIE *and* HAYDEN *stand in the same group.* MR. THORNTON *walks onto the field.*]

MR. THORNTON: Good morning! I'm Mr. Thornton, and I'm the director here. Are you all excited for football camp this week?

[*The kids cheer.*]

MR. THORNTON: Awesome! In a minute, your coaches for the week will come join you, and you all will get to practicing. Today we're mainly going to work on passing, but at the end of the week, we're going to put you on teams together and have a tournament! How does that sound?



Copyright © Mometrix Media. You have been licensed one copy of this document for personal use only. Any other reproduction or redistribution is strictly prohibited. All rights reserved.
This content is provided for test preparation purposes only and does not imply an endorsement by Mometrix of any particular political, scientific, or religious point of view.

[*The kids cheer again.* MR. THORNTON *smiles and then exits.*]
CHARLIE: Hey, it sounds like we'll only be playing against each other. So, we don't have to be worried about playing with the college players!
HAYDEN: I guess not, but I'm still a little nervous.
CHARLIE: Yeah, I'm a little nervous, too.
HAYDEN: Really? Why?
CHARLIE: Well, if they're as tall as you say they are, and they're so good at football, I'm just afraid I won't be able to keep up with them!

SCENE 3:

[*The kids are still standing in their groups. Four college football players walk onto the track, and each one walks to a different group.* JORDAN *walks over to* HAYDEN *and* CHARLIE'S *group with a football.* CHARLIE *squints his eyes at* HAYDEN, *and* HAYDEN *looks at the ground.*]
CHARLIE: [*Whispering.*] He's only a couple of feet taller than us! Why did you say they were so tall? I knew that couldn't be true.
HAYDEN: [*Whispering.*] That's how I remembered it! But I guess I was only a first grader when my parents took me to that game.
[CHARLIE *laughs and shakes his head.*]
JORDAN: Hey guys! I'm Jordan. Let's all introduce ourselves, and then after that, we'll get started!

SCENE 4:

[HAYDEN *and* CHARLIE *are standing across from each other, passing the ball back and forth.* JORDAN *walks over to them as* HAYDEN *leaps to the side to catch the ball.*]
CHARLIE: Oh, sorry! That was way off.
JORDAN: It wasn't so bad! Here, try again. Make sure you follow through after you let go of the ball.
[HAYDEN *hands the ball to* JORDAN, *who hands it to* CHARLIE. CHARLIE *passes the ball again, and* HAYDEN *easily catches it from where he stands.*]
JORDAN: See, that was great! And Hayden, that was a great catch earlier. Do either of you play on a team?
HAYDEN: No, we both want to try out for the middle school team! But we do play at recess a lot.
JORDAN: I can tell! Both of you are doing great, and by the end of the week, I'm sure you'll be even better. It may be challenging, but you are going to learn and practice a lot.
CHARLIE: [*Laughing.*] Will we practice tackling? And getting tackled?
[HAYDEN *looks away but laughs quietly.*]
JORDAN: Yeah, but don't worry, we'll put you in plenty of padding, so you'll be safe. I'm going to go help these guys. Keep up the good work!
[JORDAN *walks offstage.*]
CHARLIE: Well, it sounds like someone made a mountain out of a molehill!
HAYDEN: [*Passing the ball to* CHARLIE.] Yeah, I guess so. But I'm glad I was wrong!
[CHARLIE passes the ball back to HAYDEN.]
HAYDEN: Now I'm excited for the rest of the week. And I'm glad I get to practice with you.
CHARLIE: Yeah! It's gonna be awesome!

THE END



Copyright © Mometrix Media. You have been licensed one copy of this document for personal use only. Any other reproduction or redistribution is strictly prohibited. All rights reserved.
This content is provided for test preparation purposes only and does not imply an endorsement by Mometrix of any particular political, scientific, or religious point of view.

**28. In Scene 4, Charlie says that Hayden "made a mountain out of a molehill." What does this expression mean in the story?**

a. Hayden accomplished a very challenging task.
b. Hayden overreacted when he was worried about football camp.
c. Hayden impressed Jordan with his football skills.
d. Hayden does not want to keep practicing football with Charlie.

**29. Read Hayden's description of the college football players in Scene 1. Which of these types of stories is Hayden's description most like?**

a. A legend
b. A fable
c. A myth
d. A tall tale

**30. From the stage directions that start Scene 3, the reader can infer that:**

a. Charlie is suspicious of how Hayden had described the college football players.
b. Hayden is excited to start practicing football with Charlie.
c. Charlie is hoping to impress the college football players with his skills.
d. Hayden is upset that Charlie is better at football.

**31. What is the purpose of the anecdote that Hayden tells in Scene 1?**

a. It describes why Hayden's parents encouraged him to try football.
b. It shows that Hayden is a more experienced football player than Charlie.
c. It emphasizes how excited Hayden is for football camp.
d. It reveals why Hayden's experience has made him nervous about football camp.

*Refer to BOTH passages "Chapter 1: My Early Home" and "Football Camp" to answer questions 32-34.*

**32. What is a main difference between the narrator in "Chapter 1: My Early Home" and Hayden in "Football Camp"?**

a. The horse did not like playing with others, but Hayden was excited to play with others.
b. Hayden did not want to listen to the football coaches, but the horse listened to its mother.
c. Hayden was nervous about playing with others, but the horse was not nervous.
d. The horse found friends because he was lonely, but Hayden was not lonely.

**33. How is the narrator in "Chapter 1: My Early Home" similar to the two boys, Charlie and Hayden, in "Football Camp"?**

a. Both the horse and the boys valued the advice of their family.
b. Both the horse and the boys were afraid of the future.
c. Both the horse and the boys received guidance from someone older.
d. Both the horse and the boys learned the value of helping someone in need.

**34. Which describes a similarity between Hayden in "Football Camp" and the narrator in "Chapter 1: My Early Home"?**

a. Both had parents with respected jobs.
b. Both exaggerated their description of something they had seen.
c. Both enjoyed playing roughly with others.
d. Both describe an event that happened earlier in their childhood.



Copyright © Mometrix Media. You have been licensed one copy of this document for personal use only. Any other reproduction or redistribution is strictly prohibited. All rights reserved.
This content is provided for test preparation purposes only and does not imply an endorsement by Mometrix of any particular political, scientific, or religious point of view.

*Refer to the following for questions 35-40:*

**A Dreamer Named George Lucas**

(1) You may not know the name George Lucas, but you probably know the incredible world he created. He is the mastermind behind such beloved heroes as Luke Skywalker, R2-D2, Chewbacca, and Queen Amidala. He also created such dreaded villains as Darth Vader, Boba Fett, and Emperor Palpatine. These are some of the main characters in the wildly popular series of movies called *Star Wars*. And none of these films would exist if not for a young dreamer from Modesto, California.

(2) George Lucas was born on May 14, 1944. As a young man, George loved driving his car around Modesto and dreamed of becoming a racecar driver. However, he became interested in film while studying at junior college. He focused on film while at the University of Southern California School of Cinematic Arts, where he learned the skills that would make him famous.

(3) At the university, George made his first film. It was a science-fiction story called *THX 1138*. A friend of his thought the film was too serious. He challenged George to make a lighthearted comedy. George rose to the challenge by making a movie called *American Graffiti*. The movie was about a group of teenagers who liked nothing better than driving around town in their cars. The story was not very dramatic. The movie studio was concerned that people would not be interested in his film. But audiences related to the funny, likable characters, and the film became a big hit. George's success with *American Graffiti* meant he would be able to make more films.

(4) For his next project, he returned to science fiction. But instead of making another serious, adult film like *THX 1138*, he decided to make one with the lighthearted, fast-paced feel of *American Graffiti*. Once again, the studio executives were worried that audiences would not like George's space adventure. They thought his world of creatures and robots was too strange. Once again, the studio was wrong. Released in 1977, *Star Wars* made more money than any movie before it. George was right again.

(5) George Lucas spent the next few years working on sequels to his big hit. *The Empire Strikes Back* was released in 1980. *Return of the Jedi* followed in 1983. In the meantime, he created a new character, an adventurer named Indiana Jones. Indiana would go on to star in five popular movies of his own. It seemed that George could only have success, but making these films was a lot of hard work. He decided to take some time off from making movies, although he promised fans that there were more stories to tell in the *Star Wars* universe.

(6) Sixteen years later, George Lucas finally returned to the most successful series in movie history. But instead of picking up where *Return of the Jedi* ended, he decided to tell the story of what happened before the first *Star Wars* movie he made. *The Phantom Menace* was released in 1999. Then came *Attack of the Clones* in 2002 and *Revenge of the Sith* in 2005.

(7) When he isn't making blockbusters, George Lucas likes to spend time with his family. He even allowed his three children to appear in his most recent *Star Wars* movies. Who knows what he will dream up next?



Copyright © Mometrix Media. You have been licensed one copy of this document for personal use only. Any other reproduction or redistribution is strictly prohibited. All rights reserved.
This content is provided for test preparation purposes only and does not imply an endorsement by Mometrix of any particular political, scientific, or religious point of view.

**35. How did the author organize the information in the passage to describe George Lucas's story?**

a. By using a chronological pattern to describe George Lucas's road to success, starting with his first film in college
b. By using a compare-and-contrast pattern to describe the main characters in the *Indiana Jones* and *Star Wars* series
c. By using description to show George Lucas' creative process for thinking up new movie characters
d. By using order of importance to rank George Lucas' movies from most successful to least successful

**36. Paragraphs 3 and 4 of "A Dreamer Named George Lucas" support the key idea that:**

a. George Lucas had the goal of making movies since his childhood.
b. George Lucas did not like his film *American Graffiti.*
c. George Lucas' success with his first few movies was surprising.
d. George Lucas did not like being challenged when it came to his movie ideas.

**37. Which sentence from the passage shows that George Lucas' first *Star Wars* movie was successful?**

a. Once again, the studio executives were worried that audiences would not like George's space adventure.
b. Released in 1977, *Star Wars* made more money than any movie before it.
c. He decided to take some time off from making movies, although he promised fans that there were more stories to tell in the *Star Wars* universe.
d. But instead of picking up where *Return of the Jedi* ended, he decided to tell the story of what happened before the first *Star Wars* movie he made.

**38. What does the word *lighthearted* mean, as it is used in paragraphs 3 and 4?**

a. Fun, entertaining
b. Floating, weightless
c. Bright, colorful
d. Fragile, weak

**39. Which of the following is the best summary of "A Dreamer Named George Lucas"?**

a. George Lucas was inspired to become a filmmaker in college. Although it was hard work, he was able to make multiple movies within a few years, such as the *Star Wars* series and the *Indiana Jones* series, before taking a break. He made six *Star Wars* movies from 1977 to 2005.
b. George Lucas gave up his dream to be a racecar driver during college. After he made his first movie, a friend challenged him to make lighthearted movies. People did not think he would do well, but he was still able to make six *Star Wars* movies by the end of 2005.
c. George Lucas had creative ideas for movies. He wanted to make some about an adventurer (*Indiana Jones*) and some about space adventures (*Star Wars*). He chose to work on the *Indiana Jones* movies first because he thought they would be a big hit.
d. George Lucas studied film in college, where his comedy film, *American Graffiti*, was unexpectedly a big hit. His next film, *Star Wars*, was also an unlikely success, making more money than any other movie before it. This success led him to create many more well-known movies, such as the *Indiana Jones* movies and others in the *Star Wars* series.



Copyright © Mometrix Media. You have been licensed one copy of this document for personal use only. Any other reproduction or redistribution is strictly prohibited. All rights reserved.
This content is provided for test preparation purposes only and does not imply an endorsement by Mometrix of any particular political, scientific, or religious point of view.

**40. What is the most likely reason that the author named specific heroes and villains as film characters at the beginning of the passage, in paragraph 1?**

a. To persuade the reader that *Star Wars* is one of the best movies of all time
b. To show the reader that they may already be familiar with George Lucas' creative ideas
c. To provide a sequence of how George Lucas created each of his film characters
d. To reveal the inspirations for some of George Lucas' film characters



Copyright © Mometrix Media. You have been licensed one copy of this document for personal use only. Any other reproduction or redistribution is strictly prohibited. All rights reserved.
This content is provided for test preparation purposes only and does not imply an endorsement by Mometrix of any particular political, scientific, or religious point of view.

# Answer Key and Explanations for Test #2

**1. B:** Hobie chose baseball because his brother was already running track and he didn't want to be compared to him.

**2. A:** Twinge also means to hurt. Hobie flexed his leg so fast that it made his knee hurt a little.

**3. D:** Always being the first one to cross the finish line is a good indication that Hobie was (and still is) a good runner.

**4. A:** While Martin and Hobie may be different in many ways, they are both good at running.

**5. C:** Hobie had a hard decision to make. Forced to give up baseball, he had to choose between playing a sport where he might be compared to his brother or staying at home. Hobie found out that difficult decisions sometimes turn out all right in the end.

**6. D:** The author's step-by-step account of how Hobie made it from third to first place in the race increased the tension or suspense in the story.

**7. A:** This summary includes all the important information in the story, and is accurate.

**8. C:** Hobie's breathing became ragged because he was worn out from running so fast for so long.

**9. C:** Hobie is most likely to rejoin track the following year as a long-distance runner, an area where he showed talent. It will also allow him to avoid comparisons to his brother, who is a sprinter.

**10. D:** The speaker describes that his shadow "sometimes shoots up taller" and "sometimes gets so little." The speaker, a child, also states that the shadow does not grow "like proper children." These descriptions of the shadow show that it is not always the same size as the speaker, so choice D is incorrect. The shadow changes sizes, but the poem does not suggest that the shadow is doing this in order to tease the speaker. The shadow's motivation for changing size is not mentioned at all, so choice A is incorrect. The fact that the speaker's shadow can only being seen in the daylight is best supported later in the poem. Lines 13-16 support this by explaining that the shadow was not present in the early morning before the Sun came up. Choice B is incorrect. The speaker says that the way his shadow shrinks and grows is funny. However, the speaker does not suggest that the shadow is doing this on purpose or trying to be funny. These lines do not show that the speaker thinks the shadow is being silly, so choice C is incorrect.

**11. C:** Personification means describing something with human-like qualities. In lines 9 through 12, the speaker says that the shadow does not know how to play, embarrasses the speaker with its actions, and is a "coward" because it wants to stay close to the speaker. These lines show that the shadow is making choices that the speaker does not like. The shadow would not do these things if the speaker controlled it. This personification suggests that the shadow makes its own decisions with its own mind, so choice C is correct. These lines do not suggest that the shadow does not like the speaker, since the shadow's motivation is not explained. Choice A is incorrect. The shadow does not speak or communicate in the poem, so choice B is incorrect. Since the shadow's reason for making a fool of the speaker is not explained, the poem does not support the idea that the shadow is playing tricks. Choice D is incorrect.

**12. B, E:** Even though the shadow is not a living thing, the speaker describes his shadow as if it behaves like a person. The speaker questions some of the shadow's actions, such as how it grows



Copyright © Mometrix Media. You have been licensed one copy of this document for personal use only. Any other reproduction or redistribution is strictly prohibited. All rights reserved.
This content is provided for test preparation purposes only and does not imply an endorsement by Mometrix of any particular political, scientific, or religious point of view.

and sticks to him. The speaker also criticizes these actions, calling the shadow a coward and saying that he is not like "proper children." The reader can conclude that the speaker does not understand why his shadow behaves the way it does, so choice B is correct. Choice E is correct because the speaker calls the shadow a coward and says that it is lazy. The speaker does not suggest that he wants to befriend his shadow. In fact, the speaker complains that the shadow makes a "fool" of him, so choice A is incorrect. The speaker does not seem to worry that the shadow is lonely. Instead, the speaker calls the shadow a "coward" for sticking so closely with him all the time, so choice C is incorrect. The speaker suggests that the shadow is scared in line 11, and he does not mention being scared of the shadow, so choice D is incorrect.

**13. D:** This choice describes the shadow completing an action in the same way and at the same time as the speaker. Choice D is correct. In choice A, the speaker notes the shadow's behavior, but this does not describe how the shadow moves. This makes choice A incorrect. In choice B, the shadow "stayed behind" when the speaker got up, so the shadow did not move with the speaker. This makes choice B incorrect. Choice C describes how the shadow can suddenly grow, but not how it moves with the speaker, so it is incorrect.

**14. A:** The simile "like an India-rubber ball" is used to help the reader imagine how quickly the shadow's height increases. The shadow in the poem quickly "shoots up taller," just like a toy bouncy ball can shoot up quickly when it is bounced. The simile compares the shadow to a ball's fast movement, not a ball's round shape, so choice B is incorrect. The speaker is comparing the shadow to the ball in order to describe the shadow. The speaker is not expressing a hope that he has for the shadow, so choice C is incorrect. The simile does not demonstrate that shadows can be tinier than a toy ball because it is used to describe how the shadow "shoots up taller" and grows. Choice D is incorrect.

**15. C:** In lines 13-16, the speaker went out "before the sun was up," but his shadow "stayed at home" and "was fast asleep in bed." The speaker was up and moving, but his shadow was not with him. Shadows are created when something gets in the way of a shining light. Based on the lines in the poem and this fact about shadows, the reader can infer that the speaker's shadow cannot be seen without light. Choice C is correct. Lines 13-16 describe a time when the speaker could not see his shadow, so the reader cannot infer that the shadow can be seen at any time of day or night. This makes choice A incorrect. These lines do not describe the shadow's emotions or suggest that the shadow was upset, so choice B is incorrect. The poem does not suggest that the speaker enjoys his shadow. Additionally, the speaker calls the shadow "lazy" in line 15, which is not the same as "boring." Choice D is incorrect.

**16. A:** The word *absorb* means to soak up. When water is poured onto normal wood, the wood will soak in the water, so choice A is correct. Wood that has recently absorbed water may look darker. However, the color will eventually return to the way it was, even if there is still water in the wood. Becoming darker is one possible effect of water being absorbed, but it is not the meaning of *absorb*, so choice B is incorrect. Pouring water on wood does not cause the wood to push water away, so choice C is incorrect. The passage explains that absorbing water is different from making things stick together through cohesion, so choice D is incorrect.

**17. A:** This sentence shows that water is different from glue because it explains that water will not harden to make things stick together. This sentence contrasts the description of how glue holds things together in paragraph 3. Choice B is a sentence from the experiment. This sentence does not compare water to glue or contrast the behavior of water and glue, so it is incorrect. Choice C describes how water's atoms stick together. However, the way that glue's atoms stick together is not described in the passage. While this sentence describes a quality of water, it does not contrast it



Copyright © Mometrix Media. You have been licensed one copy of this document for personal use only. Any other reproduction or redistribution is strictly prohibited. All rights reserved.
This content is provided for test preparation purposes only and does not imply an endorsement by Mometrix of any particular political, scientific, or religious point of view.

with the qualities of glue, so choice C is incorrect. Choice D explains which atoms water is made of, but it does not describe the performance or function of water, so it is incorrect.

**18. D:** Paragraph 3 explains that glue is sticky in two ways: through adhesion and cohesion. This supports the key idea that there are multiple ways for a substance to be sticky, so choice D is correct. This idea is also supported by the passage overall, since it is about the unexpected way that water can be sticky. Paragraph 3 does not include information about whether glue is solid or liquid, so choice A is incorrect. Paragraph 3 only talks about glue. It does not talk about the chemical properties of water, so choice B is incorrect. Paragraph 3 does not talk about the purpose of water, so choice C is incorrect.

**19. C:** The experiment instructions caution readers against throwing pennies in. The instructions say to slip the pennies in gently and avoid creating a splash, so the reader can conclude that splashing could affect the results of the experiment. The reader cannot conclude that other liquids would behave in the same way as water, especially because water is described as a unique substance in paragraph 4, so choice A is incorrect. The reader cannot conclude that the same number of pennies will make the water spill each time. The experiment directions say that usually it takes more than 10 pennies, and that a scientist was able to put in 25 pennies. This shows the reader that the number of pennies that result in a spill may vary, so choice B is incorrect. Glue and water are described in paragraph 2 as being sticky in different ways. The passage also does not suggest that glue and water are similar, so the reader cannot conclude that glue is made of the same elements as water. This makes choice D incorrect.

**20. D:** The passage first describes the properties of water and then describes an experiment that demonstrates the stickiness of water. Someone would not normally expect water, which we encounter in our everyday lives, to be sticky. However, the information in the passage and shows why water can be considered sticky. The passage does not describe multiple science experiments or explain how safe they are, so choice A is incorrect. The main idea of the passage is about water, not glue. Glue is simply used as an example that is compared to water, so choice B is incorrect. Water being used to wash away stickiness does show water's qualities, but the use of water to wash things is not the main idea of the passage, so choice C is incorrect.

**21. C:** Paragraphs 3 and 4 show that water and glue are sticky in different ways by comparing their qualities. Paragraphs 3 and 4 do not describe different uses for water, so choice A is incorrect. Paragraphs 3 and 4 do not describe what to do with water in the experiment. That information is given later in the passage, so choice B is incorrect. Water's washing qualities are mentioned in the first paragraph. The purpose of this passage is to inform, not persuade. Additionally, this information does help the reader understand that water itself is sticky, so choice D is incorrect.

**22. C:** The author explains the sticky qualities of water by defining cohesion. The author also provides instructions for an experiment that show how water will stick to itself. This shows that choice C is correct. The passage does not provide a sequence of events or explain how the stickiness of water was discovered, so choice A is incorrect. The passage is not written in order to argue that water is the most unique substance. The passage includes facts that make water unique, but this is not the main topic of the passage, so choice B is incorrect. The passage does not contain information about other experiments, so choice D is incorrect.

**23. B:** The section explains that when each penny is added to the water, the water molecules pack together and hold on to each other because of cohesion. This happens because of the water's properties, so it is not caused by the pennies. This supports the inference that the experiment could be done with other small objects. This section does not discuss glue or suggest that glue does not



Copyright © Mometrix Media. You have been licensed one copy of this document for personal use only. Any other reproduction or redistribution is strictly prohibited. All rights reserved.
This content is provided for test preparation purposes only and does not imply an endorsement by Mometrix of any particular political, scientific, or religious point of view.

have cohesion, which makes choice A incorrect. This section says that the experiment can be done more than once. It also says that the number of pennies that can be added is not always the same. This describes the same experiment, but does not introduce other experiments, so choice C is incorrect. In paragraph 3, the properties of cohesion and adhesion are explained as two different things, not the same thing. Additionally, this section does not mention adhesion, so choice D is incorrect.

**24. B:** The bullet points list the four items needed to complete the experiment. This list helps the reader understand what they will need to gather before starting the experiment. The text after each bullet point names an item needed for the experiment, but it does not tell the reader how to use the item. The text does not provide step-by-step instructions, so choice A is incorrect. The text in the list does not include similes that help the reader understand how molecules look, so choice C is incorrect. The information in the list does not show how safe or easy the experiment is, as the list only contains the supplies that are needed for the experiment. The list does not describe the actual experiment, so choice D is incorrect.

**25. C:** The passage says that the horse's mother would leave to work during the day. Later, in paragraph 6, the horse's mother tells him that the cart-horse colts have not learned manners. This shows that the narrator's mother does not work as a cart-horse, so the horses in the meadow must have different jobs. Choice C is correct. The passage only states that the horse's grandfather had won races. The reader cannot infer that the horse's mother and father have also won races, so choice A is incorrect. The passage does not suggest that the young colts did not like the narrator. The young colts play roughly, but this is because they have not learned manners. Choice B is incorrect. Only the reader narrator's mother gives advice in this passage. The only fact the passage gives about the narrator's father is that he is well respected, so choice D is incorrect.

**26. D:** In choice D, the narrator's mother is describing the other colts to him. She says that they are cart-horse colts and that they do not have manners. The narrator's mother warns him about the cart-horse colts and compares him to them. This shows that the narrator is different from the other colts, so choice D is correct. Choice A describes the narrator. However, the passage does not say that the other colts did not do this. This is normal for a young horse, so choice A is incorrect. Choice B also does not explain a difference between the narrator and other horses in the meadow. It focuses on the narrator's mother, so choice B is incorrect. Choice C explains how the narrator played with the young colts but does not describe a difference between them, so it is incorrect.

**27. B:** The author begins the story by describing the nature and surroundings of the narrator's first home. This allows the reader to picture what the setting looked like, so choice B is correct. This paragraph does not describe any of the horses. It only describes the meadow where the horses live. Paragraph 6 explains why the narrator was different from the other colts in the meadow, not paragraph 1, so choice A is incorrect. Paragraph 4 explains how the narrator played with the other horses, not paragraph 1, so choice C is incorrect. In paragraph 1, the narrator calls the meadow "pleasant," and he does not suggest that he no longer wants to live in the meadow. Choice D is incorrect.

**28. B:** The expression "make a mountain out of a molehill" is a common adage that means someone made a big deal out of something small. Hayden was nervous all week about playing football with college athletes and being tackled. However, Hayden finds that reality is not as bad as he feared it would be, and the college players were not as scary as he remembered, so choice B is correct. The expression does not refer to Hayden accomplishing a challenging task, so choice A is incorrect. It also does not refer to Hayden impressing Jordan with his football skills, as Jordan was also



Copyright © Mometrix Media. You have been licensed one copy of this document for personal use only. Any other reproduction or redistribution is strictly prohibited. All rights reserved.
This content is provided for test preparation purposes only and does not imply an endorsement by Mometrix of any particular political, scientific, or religious point of view.

impressed with Charlie, so choice C is incorrect. Hayden is glad to practice football with Charlie, so choice D is incorrect.

**29. D:** In Scene 1, Hayden claims that the football players are three times as tall as he and Charlie are. This is most like a tall tale because Hayden's description is an exaggerated, and not likely possible, version of something that really happened. Therefore, choice D is correct. A legend is a story that has been passed down within a certain culture. Usually, legends are used to explain something that happened long ago, and they cannot be proven true or false. Choice A is incorrect since Hayden's story is not passed down and his claim is proven false. Fables usually teach a lesson or moral. Hayden's description does not teach a lesson, so choice B is incorrect. Myths are usually used to explain a supernatural event or why something in nature exists. Since Hayden's description does not refer to a supernatural event or the reason for something in nature, choice C is incorrect.

**30. A:** The stage directions in Scene 3 have four college football players walk out onto the track, including Jordan walking over to Hayden and Charlie's group. The reader can infer that Charlie squints his eyes at Hayden because seeing the football players up close reveals that they are not three times as tall as the boys, as Hayden had described in an earlier scene. The setting and body language given in the scene show that Charlie is suspicious of what Hayden has told him because it ends up being false information, so choice A is correct. There is nothing in the stage directions that suggests that Hayden is excited in this scene, so choice B is incorrect. The stage directions do not suggest that Charlie is hoping to impress the college football players with his skills, so choice C is incorrect. While the stage directions state that Hayden looks at the ground, this is not because he is upset about Charlie being better at football, so choice D is incorrect.

**31. D:** Hayden's anecdote in Scene 1 describes the college football players he saw as being "three times as tall" as him. This explains why Hayden is nervous about going to football camp, so choice D is correct. Hayden's fear creates the story's conflict, so this anecdote is important to the story. In the anecdote, Hayden mentions that his parents took him to a football game. However, these events do not explain why Hayden's parents encouraged him to try football, so choice A is incorrect. The anecdote does not show that Hayden is more experienced at football than Charlie, only that he has been to a game, so choice B is incorrect. The anecdote shows why Hayden is nervous about football camp, not how excited he is, so choice C is incorrect.

**32. C:** Hayden was nervous about playing with others at football camp, specifically because he feared playing against college football players and getting tackled. The horse, however, was not nervous about playing with others, so choice C is correct. The passage says he had "great fun" running and playing with the other horses, so choice A is incorrect. Hayden does not show a desire to disobey or ignore the football coaches, so choice B is incorrect. The horse does not say he is lonely or act like he is lonely, which means that choice D is unsupported by the passage and is incorrect.

**33. C:** The horse received guidance from his mother on how to play with the other horses. The boys received guidance from Jordan when they practiced passing the football. These events show that choice C is correct. Only the horse receives advice from family in the passage. The boys do not interact with their family members in the play, so choice A is incorrect. The horse does not show any worry about the future in the passage, so choice B is incorrect. Neither the horse nor the boys learned the value of helping someone in need, so choice D is incorrect.

**34. D:** Both Hayden and the horse describe an event that happened earlier in their childhood. Hayden describes the game that his parents took him to, and the horse describes playing with the other horses and being cared for by his mother. This shows that choice D is correct. "Chapter 1: My



Copyright © Mometrix Media. You have been licensed one copy of this document for personal use only. Any other reproduction or redistribution is strictly prohibited. All rights reserved.
This content is provided for test preparation purposes only and does not imply an endorsement by Mometrix of any particular political, scientific, or religious point of view.

Early Home" says that the horse's mother has a job and is valued by their owner. However, "Football Camp" does not state what Hayden's parents' jobs are, so choice A is incorrect. Hayden exaggerated his description when telling Charlie about the football players. However, the horse does not use an exaggeration to describe anything, so choice B is incorrect. The horse enjoyed playing roughly with the colts, but Hayden was worried about playing roughly with others. This makes choice C incorrect.

**35. A:** The passage uses a chronological pattern and tells the events that led to George Lucas's success as a filmmaker, so choice A is correct. The passage does not contain specific information that compares and contrasts the main characters in George Lucas' various movies, so choice B is incorrect. The passage does not describe George Lucas's process for creating new movie characters, so choice C is incorrect. The information in the passage lists George Lucas' movies after *Star Wars* in the order they were made. It does not list them in order of most successful to least successful, so choice D is incorrect.

**36. C:** Paragraphs 3 and 4 support the idea that the success of George Lucas' first few movies was surprising. Paragraph 3 says that "the movie studio was concerned that people would not be interested" in his film *American Graffiti*. Paragraph 4 says that "the studio executives were worried that audiences would not like George's space adventure." Despite this, each film became a hit. George Lucas's first interest in film is explained in paragraph 2. Paragraphs 3 and 4 do not mention any of George Lucas's childhood goals, so choice A is incorrect. Paragraphs 3 and 4 do not describe George Lucas's opinion of his films. They suggest that he was more interested in science fiction than realistic fiction. However, this does not support the idea that he did not like *American Graffiti*, so choice B is incorrect. Paragraph 3 explains that George Lucas "rose to the challenge" to make a lighthearted comedy instead of a serious film. This shows that George Lucas accepted the challenge and tried something new. The passage does not show that he did not like to be challenged on his ideas, so choice D is incorrect.

**37. B:** This sentence clearly shows the success of George Lucas' first *Star Wars* movie by explaining that the movie made more money than any movie before it. The movie would not have made so much money if it had not attracted a large audience, so choice B is correct. Choice A shows that the studio executives thought George Lucas' movie would not be successful. This does not show the result of the movie's release, so choice A is incorrect. Choice C shows that the *Star Wars* series had many interested fans. However, it does not mention the success of George Lucas' first *Star Wars* movie, so it is incorrect. Choice D explains what George Lucas did after taking a break from making movies. This sentence does not show how successful the first *Star Wars* movie was, so choice D is incorrect.

**38. A:** The word *lighthearted* describes something that is fun and entertaining. Paragraph 3 supports this by describing *American Graffiti* as a "lighthearted comedy" with characters that are "funny" and "likable." The word *lighthearted* is also used in contrast to George Lucas' first film, which was "too serious." Even though *lighthearted* has the word *light* in it, the passage does not mention weight or describe floating, so choice B is incorrect. The word *lighthearted* is used to describe the mood of two of George Lucas' movies, not colors, so choice C is incorrect. Nothing in paragraphs 3 and 4 is described as fragile, weak, or anything similar, so choice D is incorrect.

**39. D:** Choice D includes key ideas from the beginning, middle, and end of the passage. This summary does not include unnecessary details, and it reflects the main idea of the passage. Choice A does not mention the movies that led George Lucas to make *Star Wars.* This information is a key idea in the passage, so choice A is incorrect. Choice B is incorrect because it does not mention the success of *American Graffiti* or *Star Wars*. The success of George Lucas's movies is a key idea in the



Copyright © Mometrix Media. You have been licensed one copy of this document for personal use only. Any other reproduction or redistribution is strictly prohibited. All rights reserved.
This content is provided for test preparation purposes only and does not imply an endorsement by Mometrix of any particular political, scientific, or religious point of view.

passage, so it should be included in the summary. Choice C is also missing these key ideas. Additionally, this summary is inaccurate because the passage states that George Lucas made the first *Star Wars* movie before he created the *Indiana Jones* movie character. Choice C is incorrect.

**40. B:** The author names a variety of characters in the *Star Wars* movie series in paragraph 1. With this list, the author explains that although the readers may not know of George Lucas, they have probably heard of some of his well-known heroes and villains. Choice B is correct. The author does not argue or attempt to persuade the reader that *Star Wars* is one of the best movies of all time, so choice A is incorrect. Paragraph 1 does not describe the chronological order in which George Lucas created the characters in *Star Wars*, so choice C is incorrect. Paragraph 1 only names some of George Lucas' most well-known movie characters. It does not reveal what inspired him to create these characters, so choice D is incorrect.



Copyright © Mometrix Media. You have been licensed one copy of this document for personal use only. Any other reproduction or redistribution is strictly prohibited. All rights reserved.
This content is provided for test preparation purposes only and does not imply an endorsement by Mometrix of any particular political, scientific, or religious point of view.

## Online Resources

Due to our efforts to try to keep this book to a manageable length, we've created a link that will give you access to all of your online resources:

mometrix.com/resources719/vsolg5read

# It's Your Moment, Let's Celebrate It!

Share your story @mometrixtestpreparation



Copyright © Mometrix Media. You have been licensed one copy of this document for personal use only. Any other reproduction or redistribution is strictly prohibited. All rights reserved.
This content is provided for test preparation purposes only and does not imply an endorsement by Mometrix of any particular political, scientific, or religious point of view.